WISE TALK

from the

OTHER SIDE

A Journey To the Heart of Love

BY HEATHER CRISWELL

Published by WiseInside® www.wiseinside.com

WiseInside
wisdom shared from the inside out

Contact the author at heather@wiseinside.com

ISBN-13: 978-0692726181
ISBN-10: 0692726187

Printed in the United States of America

First Edition

CONTENTS

IN THE BEGINNING

I remember as a young child I knew I was special. I felt it in my soul. I felt a light that would beam from my chest and spread love in a way uniquely my own. I felt important. I knew I was good. I felt that love was mine to have and give.

In fact, as a young lady being raised in the Catholic Church, I was taught to confess my sins to our priest. I remember standing in line and telling my friends I thought it was a dumb idea. I said, "Why do I need to confess anything? I'm a really good kid." Their response was, "You better do it or you are going to get in trouble." So I sat down across from the priest, 5 or 6 years old, and proceeded to lie by making up a sin. I told the priest I stole something and he told me to say my "Hail Mary's" and off I went. I felt no desire to say "Hail Mary's" and in that moment, I decided the church was not for me.

I knew. I knew there was no need to confess anything. I believed in my greatness.

And then I went to school. I began to forget. There were so many kids (and adults) that chipped away at the love I had for myself (and humanity). I was a fat kid, in the 70's, in the South. I actually started school when I was four because my parents knew I was much bigger than most of my friends. They were doing their best to save me from embarrassment and humiliation. It was bound to happen. Even though I started early, I was the biggest, fattest kid in my class . . . every year. You can find me in the school pictures dead center on the top row, usually with some ridiculous hairstyle and unflattering clothes that made me feel even more awkward in my body.

For as long as I can remember, I was bullied. More than bullied, it was torture. From the minute I got on the bus in the morning, until the minute I finally set foot in my home in the afternoon . . . constant chipping. Chipping away at my soul.

As the bus pulled up to my stop, a boy would begin screaming, "Everyone hold on, Heather, Heather... not light as a feather... is getting on. Hold on, the whale is going to take us down."

Every. Single. Day.

The "luck of the draw" put the same boy in my homeroom

class and the majority of my other classes throughout the day. He would get the other children in class to do their share of chipping too.

Every. Single. Day.

The bus ride home was always full of verbal assaults. Usually followed up with "Run home fatty. Oh, you can't run. Walk home to the three little pigs' house." (Yes, it was a perfect storm. My parents were overweight too.)

Every. Single. Day.

I started to forget my greatness. Everyday a piece of me would disappear. I would replace the piece with food, hoping that it would make me feel better. I felt worse. It got worse.

Over time my mother noticed. She recognized my light going dim.

One night she came into my room early to kiss me goodnight. I was sobbing. The ugly cry. The cry we have all had at some point in time. The cry that forces us to visit the dark side in our mind and ask ourselves the questions that go against everything we are born to believe.

Why am I here? Why do I exist? Would the world be better off without me? Wouldn't it be easier to leave? Why does it hurt so much? Am I really that disgusting? What if it never stops? What if they are right? What if every thing they say is true?

I confessed. I told her all the humiliating, embarrassing, destructive, abusive, and painful experiences I had been enduring over time. I felt terrible. And, I felt relief. Finally someone knew all my pain. Shame. Humiliation. Embarrassment.

My mother was WiseInside. She knew what to do. She started by telling me a story. The story was my own story. She wanted to remind me. Remind me of my worthiness. My value. She reminded me that I was a miracle. Born on purpose... for a purpose.

She told me to scoot over and grabbed my hand, wiped away my tears, and started:

"You were never 'supposed' to be born. I had cervical cancer and they removed part of my cervix at 16 years old. The doctors told me I would never be able to have children. I would never be able to conceive. And if, by some miracle, I did conceive, I would never be able to carry a child to full term."

"I met your father and we made peace with the idea that children were not going to be in our future. We decided to be truck drivers and see the country. We were scheduled to look at a couple of big rigs and I was feeling very sick. I went to the doctor and found out I was pregnant with you. They said I needed to be prepared to lose the baby. I needed to know I would miscarry. I was struggling with the pregnancy the entire time."

"Around the 4th month I went to the hospital with terrible pains and I knew I was in trouble. The doctors found out you had a twin and we had lost that baby. You were still alive and your twin actually helped keep you alive. They sent me home and said it would all probably end soon. You were determined. You came 2 weeks late and weighed in at 10 pounds 4 ounces. They actually had to pull you out with forceps because you wanted to stay in my belly. You were healthy. You were alive. You were born on purpose, for a purpose. You were my miracle."

She looked me in the eyes and said something that made me remember: "They are wrong."

And just like that, I was reminded of my light. My greatness. My value. I remembered I mattered.

I still endured the bullying.

Every. Single. Day.

It was different, though. Because every time they chipped away at me I recalled the simple sentence my mother said, "They are wrong."

I believed her. Not because she was my mom, but because she sparked that wisdom within me, the knowing we all come to this planet with. She inspired me to see my greatness. To reconnect with that great source of light and love and claim it as my own, again.

The challenges of life didn't get easier. In fact, it was about to get a lot harder. The school bully was a warm up act for the real show called life.

When my grandfather hit me in the stomach and said, "You will never be a model with a gut like that," I forgot.

When my first boyfriend told me I needed to lose weight to be with him, I forgot.

When I wasn't hired because I wouldn't "represent the company's values," I forgot.

When my fiancé cheated on me with a girl half my size, I forgot.

When my dad said, "You're going to get diabetes just like your mom and me because you are so fat," I forgot.

When the seat belt on the Superman ride at Six Flags didn't fit, I forgot.

When the guys at the bar lied and used me, I forgot.

When I cried myself to sleep, feeling like I would never have a husband or a family, I forgot.

With each experience, it was more and more difficult to remember I was a miracle.

But each time I would pick myself up, dust myself off, go eat a cookie, and start again. I would remind myself that they were wrong. Often it was within a few hours or days. Sometimes it took a month or even a year to remember. Remembering saved my life more times than I wish to admit, and has inspired me to be the best version of myself, to remember I am, truly, WiseInside.

I believe we call our experiences into our lives. We are given the opportunity from our family members, friends, co-workers, children, and even the stranger at the gas station, to reconnect to our greatness.

It can show up as contrast and be extremely painful. When my fiancé cheated on me, I felt that I was not enough. I felt like my grandfather was right, no one would ever love me as a fat ass. And I kept telling myself they were wrong. I deserved to be loved. I deserved to be in a relationship that didn't hurt me like that. I reconnected to my own wisdom and filled my body with love (and cookies!). I left the relationship knowing that this was all in my highest good. It hurt. A lot. But it felt good to remember.

Sometimes the loving reminder we need most is delivered by an Earth Angel. Someone who sees our greatness when all we feel is despair. I was so sad in my sophomore year of high school. I didn't have a boyfriend. I didn't have a lot of friends. I was still experiencing more bullying than I care to remember. My Uncle Ronnie was at our house and found me crying. I told him that no one would ever love me. I was too ugly and questioned (yet again) why I was even here on this planet. He said to me, "Come on, let's go get some cookies." (Seriously, I can't make this up.)

We got in the car and went to the local gas station that served hot Otis Spunkmeyer cookies. We loaded up. We didn't wait to get home. We ate every single one in the car. We had a conversation that I will never forget. He reminded me of everything that was brilliant, beautiful, and wonderful about me. He reminded me this was just a moment in time, and all would be well. I made him promise me he was telling me the truth. He said, "I wouldn't lie to you about this. I promise you will have a beautiful husband who loves you and cares for you just as you are. He will see the beauty in you and outside of you. I promise."

And with that the radio played Marky Mark and the Funky Bunch "Good Vibrations." My Uncle said, "Turn this up. This is a great song!"

He danced in the front seat, singing at the top of his lungs, "It's such a good vibration, it's such a sweet sensation." We both danced and sang our hearts out. He helped me remember that wisdom within, the knowing that all is well. I am enough.

Each time life throws me a challenge, it's an opportunity to reconnect to love. Love for myself, first. Love for life. Love for humanity.

We come to this planet with a knowing, an inner wisdom, an intuition, a gut feeling beyond any explanation or description. It can only be felt. It is an infinite wisdom that we carry into this body for us to call on, confide in, and trust to guide us through this journey we call life.

We know. We know our worth. We know our value. We

know we matter.

We are connected to a great source of light and love. Born to care and share, be kind, compassionate and empathetic, authentic and full of purpose, successful, and above all … centered in love. It's not something we need to be taught, it's something we have.

As time goes by, we begin to forget. We forget we are amazing human beings, full of wisdom and love. Sometimes our environment helps us to forget. Often the people in our lives help us forget. We begin to believe we're not worthy, that we have to earn our place in this world and prove our worth. Over time we begin to believe we're simply not enough.

It's much easier to connect to that love and wisdom when we have supportive, inspiring, and loving family members to help us remember our greatness.

Through all the bullying, all the times I felt I would never be enough, I was blessed with an amazing family, small in size, big in heart. They infused my being with a million reasons why I was meant to be here. They stopped at nothing to show me that I mattered.

But life threw me a curveball I never anticipated: Losing

my entire family - and future family - over a span of 12 years. I barely had time to breathe between each passing. I lost every family member I had.

Mom. Dad. Grandparents. Babies. Pets. Gone.

Everyone. Gone.

I felt like a boxer in the ring of life. I'd take a hit and fall to the mat, over and over again. I'd struggle to stand up and stumble across the ring trying to get my footing, only to be knocked down again. Eventually, when everyone I loved was gone, I was left in the ring, knocked out and completely alone.

All I could feel was sadness. Grief. Anger. Loss.

I was alone.

I wanted to throw in the towel. I was done.

Until the day I connected with my loved ones beyond the physical world. This experience changed everything. I was able to shift my perceptions. I could hear, feel and sense them on the other side. (I will go more into the specifics of this experience in the last chapter, The Roundtable.) They explained the journey through this life, how the suffering we experience, the sadness we feel, and the sickness we endure, all lead to love.

They even described this book in detail for me. I was encouraged to sit down at my computer, light some candles, and write a chapter for each family member to share our life's story together. Each family member I lost has a chapter, ordered in the same way they left this planet. Their wisdom is sprinkled throughout each dedicated chapter, inspired and written with the words whispered in my ear and felt in my heart.

This book takes you on a journey. Death. Grief. Loss. Laughter. Sadness. Inspiration. Divorce. Miscarriage. Anger. Faith. Shame. Hope. Always ending in Love.

The greatest gift this book has given me is the opportunity to see love when all I could feel was pain. It has empowered me to step back and hear the truth from the other side. To stop crying. Start breathing. Start feeling. Start living.

My hope for you is that you see the possibility for love in every experience, know you are WiseInside and become inspired to seek the wisdom and love that surrounds you, both in this world and worlds beyond.

Our journey in this life always circles back to Love. It's

here for you. Always.

PAPA BILL

William J. Aumiller: The Architect
Maternal Grandfather

The world knew him as William J Aumiller, but to me, he was my Papa Bill. He was so much more than I ever knew. A brilliant architect hired to design buildings, homes, and gorgeous Catholic churches in Texas. I was so young, I just knew I wasn't allowed to sit at the big rectangle table (his drafting table) and I had to keep my hands away from his special erasers.

He was such a jolly soul. Kinda like Santa Claus, but without the beard. He was short and round and super comfy to snuggle with.

I was never denied the opportunity to sit in his lap and hang out with him. My mom would say, "Heather Reneé, get off of your Grandpa. You are going to crush his legs. You are too heavy." He would simply say, "Nonsense. She is perfect. She's perfectly fine exactly where she is."

Then he would whisper in my ear, "She's just jealous. She wishes she could sit in my lap but she is really old, she would squish me for sure." I instantly felt supported, accepted, and loved. We would have a secret chuckle and exchange a look of immeasurable love.

Papa Bill's Wisdom: A little discomfort in my legs isn't worth a lifetime of discomfort for a young, overweight girl. It was never about her weight. She needed someone she trusted to say, "She's wrong. It's not true." She needed to experience a shift from shame and embarrassment to laughter, acceptance, and love. Instantly.

Papa Bill married my Grandma Hazel. They were my mother's parents. They struggled as a couple, I never really knew the details but they divorced when my mother was 16 years old. At some point in time, they reconciled and actually remarried. But it didn't last long at all. I never witnessed my maternal Grandfather and Grandmother together as a couple.

I only knew him when he was with "Grandma Margaret." She wasn't well liked by the family. I'm not really sure why, other than she was my Grandfather's new wife. She wasn't very warm and fuzzy, but she was always kind to me. There was a noticeable tension in the family when she was present, a constant, unwavering tension.

My grandfather was pretty close to my mother. They had a strong bond and deeply loved each other. He always wanted the best for our family. Like when my parents were looking to buy a house in Conroe, Texas. My parents, in all their wisdom, decided it would be great to move their four-year-old daughter to a retirement community in the middle of nowhere … thanks guys. He said he could do better.

He decided to build a house for us.

While they were building our house, he asked me what color carpet I wanted. My immediate answer (of course): Pink! When they completed the house my parents walked into my room and onto the Pepto-Bismol pink carpet. They scolded my Grandpa for the carpet installers' mistake. He simply replied, "There's no mistake. I asked Heather what color she wanted and she said pink. So she got pink." My mother said, "This looks hideous! The rest of the house has brown carpet and then you walk in here and it looks like Barbie threw up."

All he said was, "It's a good thing there is a door. You can always shut it. The carpet stays." And that was that. Done. At four years old, I was heard, acknowledged, and granted pink carpet.

Papa Bill's Wisdom: Give children the opportunity to make a decision - an important decision - for themselves. Honor their choice and know that this experience will remind them in the future they always have a choice. And most of all, don't sweat the small stuff. Just shut the door if you don't like it.

He loved the house he designed and built so much that he bought the property next door to our house and built the exact same house for himself and his wife.

It was a challenge living in a retirement community as a four-year-old. There were no kids. Period. My mother would "ship in" family friends to spend the night, but most of the time it was just my mom and me. My father worked several hours away in Houston and was only home on the weekends.

The best part was living next door to a Grandfather that only saw the best in me. Always. My mom would make me mad and I would run to his house to be "saved." (To be fair, I drove her absolutely insane most of the time. Karma is coming back around with my own son. Ha!)

Papa Bill always took my side. He never questioned my

stories. He just loved me through it. Believing in me. Whispering so much love in my ear.

Papa Bill's Wisdom: Be a safe place to fall for the little souls in your life. We don't always have to have a "teachable" moment. Sometimes it just needs to be a loveable moment. Lighten up. It's just not that serious.

He was pretty overweight and out of shape for as long as I can remember. He had diabetes and was overall in poor physical health. Grandma Margaret would do her best to keep him in line and restrict him, but he always found a way to get what he wanted. And it usually involved me!

I remember the big white round bucket chair he would sit in to watch television. He would call me over to tell me a secret. He whispered in my ear, "Do you want to go on a treasure hunt?" I would simply nod my head, we had to be quiet so we wouldn't get caught. He said, "Go out to my truck and under the seat where the steering wheel is you will find a Snickers candy bar. Now get the bar, hide it in your shirt, and run over to me. Whatever you do, don't let Grandma Margaret see the candy. She will take it away from both of us. We don't want that. Do you think you can do it?"

I knew the drill. I would quietly nod, resolutely shake my

head in agreement and begin my mission: get the candy bar so we can both eat it. (He always shared the loot.) I ran outside, found the bar, and ran back in, past my Grandma. It was squishy from the heat, melting quickly, but that didn't matter. He would take a bite and then give me a bite. Grandma Margaret would walk in the room and he would slide it down the chair until she passed.

It was sneaky. It was fun. It was our little game. It was our special connection. It certainly wasn't the best food choice, but it was never about the food. It was about us. Feeling connected. Sharing fun. Having secrets. Loving life ... together.

Papa Bill's Wisdom: Not all secrets are bad. Sometimes we need someone to share special moments and inside jokes with, to laugh with when no one else is looking. Trust your gut, you will know when it doesn't feel right. You will know. Also be open to the good secrets, the ones that leave a love stamp on your heart. There is more good than bad, promise.

After I found the "treasure" in my Grandpa's truck, I thought ALL trucks had treasures under the driver's seat. So I proceeded to take everything out from under my father's truck seat looking for Snickers bars. My parents asked what I was up to. I told them I was looking for treasure. Little did I know that I was actually ratting out my Grandpa!

Even though he was often "caught" he never gave up. He would whisper in my ear, "Heather, go ask Grandma Margaret for some pretzels." (Pretzels were his weakness and guilty pleasure.) I didn't like pretzels, but that didn't matter. I would ask my Grandma and she would say, "Did your Papa Bill put you up to this?" I would look back at him patiently waiting in the living room and shake my head saying, "No ma'am." She would give me a bowl of pretzels and off I went. I'm pretty sure she knew what was going on, but she let it slide, allowing us the enjoyment of our little game.

Papa Bill was a kind, gentle soul. The talents he shared with the world will live on forever. He built homes for families to share love in, buildings to house companies, and churches for people to worship in for years to come.

He never really spoke of God or spirituality. He just oozed love. Pure, authentic, compassionate Love.

He reminded me of my greatness, even when others would forget.

Papa Bill's Wisdom: Follow your calling. Know that your

talents and gifts are uniquely your own. There will never be another YOU on this planet. You don't get to call it big or small, a calling is a purpose that needs to be honored. It's your unique way of spreading love and light on this planet. We need you. We want you. You matter. Your light matters.

After living in a retirement community for a couple of years, my father enduring a terrible commute, and my mother losing her mind with me at home all day everyday, my parents decided to sell our home.

I was so sad. Even at a young age I knew I would never have the time I spent with my Grandpa again. I knew I would miss him, terribly. It would never be the same again.

We would see my Papa Bill on major holidays and special occasions, but it was different. He was getting older and just seemed tired.

When I was nine years old on a family vacation exploring Colorado, my mother went to a payphone at the campground and called home to check in. She came back to the camper, in complete shock, and told my dad we had to go home now. She booked a flight back to Houston and left my dad and me to drive home. Papa Bill had suffered massive strokes and they didn't know if he would make it.

After residing in the hospital for months, he survived to live out a couple more years. But it wasn't pretty.

He was in rehabilitation and seemed to be getting better. Although it was a challenge to understand him, he could still talk. We were hopeful, optimistic, and prayed for healing.

It just got worse. He suffered more strokes, completely paralyzing his broken body. We communicated through our eyes. One blink for "no," two blinks for "yes." It was painful to watch. His mind was there, but his body would not respond. I would hold his hand and watch a single tear roll down his face. I knew. I knew we were on borrowed time. I knew there would be no more treasure hunts.

A great soul was getting ready to leave.

Papa Bill's Wisdom: Sometimes we choose a death that looks bad or seems to have so much suffering. When really the intention is to give everyone an opportunity to make peace with the transition and allows the one leaving, the option to stay. The choice is yours. Always.

It was a Saturday night, eight days before my birthday. My mom was headed to Conroe to see my grandfather. I was vacuuming our house when the phone rang. My father walked down the hall and said, "Doodle, your Papa Bill just died." A piece of me died that day. My cheerleader. My teammate. My friend. My Papa Bill was gone.

In his last moments, something amazing happened. His wife and nurses said that when he took his last breath, he reached up to the sky and then wrapped his arms around himself hugging and smiling. For a year and a half prior to that moment, he had been paralyzed, completely bedridden, and unable to communicate other than blinking his eyes. It was his gift to us.

Papa Bill's Wisdom: You are so much more than your physical body. Our thoughts and beliefs often get in the way of recognizing magical, miracle moments. Know that we choose everything. How we live. How we die. Our choices have more purpose than you know. It's not all bad, what seems "bad" is often just necessary to achieve the desired outcome. We are capable of far more than you believe. You have more power than you think you do. When we open our minds and our hearts, the possibilities are endless. Promise.

Over the next few weeks, stories started circulating in our family. Stories that my grandfather had "visited" one of the young distant cousins. The boy was four years old and told stories of my grandfather he was too young to have experienced.

My grandfather's death opened my eyes to the wonders of the "other side." I would tell stories at slumber parties as a child to prove that there was life after death. These were my own versions of "ghost stories."

Papa Bill's Wisdom: The little souls on the planet are still connected to divine wisdom. They have open eyes, ears, and hearts. Please listen, connect, and believe them when they tell you about a "ghost." Trust that there is more than meets the eyes. Trust the little ones, for they are the ones who have it right.

I was 11 when my grandfather passed away. Although I was sad he was gone, I loved that he was not here suffering and that he was "living" on the other side. There was beauty in his story. There was hope, actual proof, that we are more than our physical bodies and there's more to come when we leave them.

I remembered the beauty of my grandfather's story and told it as often as possible. Eventually, over time, the story faded. And after living life, death became a pretty bad option. I forgot the beauty of it and for the next 14 years, I was spared the experience of a loved one's passing.

Papa Bill's Wisdom: All is well, sweet child. You can call on me anytime. I am here. I am with you more than you know. I am guiding you, holding your hand when you cry, whispering in your ear when you lose all hope. Whispering with love, "We need you. We want you. You matter. Promise."

GRANDMA HAZEL

Hazel Aumiller: The Southern Lady
Maternal Grandmother

Hazel Aumiller was the definition of a gen-u-ine Southern Lady: polite, dressed to impress, a little bit of sass, and a whole lot of charm. But don't you dare mistake her manners and charm as a weakness.

She just happened to work in the Texas steel industry led by the "Good Ol' Boys." She started in a time where the woman's place (especially in the South) was in the home.

She worked her way up the ladder and ended up being the accounts receivable manager for the entire steel group. (You know, the person responsible for getting everyone to pay in a timely fashion: the bill collector!) Employed by the same company for over 45 years, she was actually working from her home the day she died at 79 years old. (She was the only one that could get the old, long standing accounts to pay.) She was a genius. Powerful. Ladylike. Sophisticated. Authentic.

Grandma Hazel's Wisdom: There's no need to protest to get what you want. Often, the back door approach is easier. You will get your way. Sometimes it just takes a little sugar and spice and everything nice. There's no need to compromise YOU. That's just not necessary to get what you want. Put your red lipstick on, wear what feels good, and own your space. You have the right to take up space. You have the right to share YOU with the world. Stand in your power with kindness and love in your heart and courage and strength in your mind. This is all yours for the taking.

Although I sensed she was important at work, to me, she was just my Grandma. And her work was just a place where my mom dropped me off so I could catch a ride with Grandma to her farm about an hour and a half away in the small Texas town, Needville.

The farm was built and designed by my Papa Bill during their marriage reconciliation period. After the house and farm were built, my Papa Bill left and my Grandma Hazel lived there for the rest of her life. Alone. (I'm pretty sure she liked it that way.)

Going to the farm didn't happen as much as I wanted, but when it did, it was magical. From the minute we got in the car, it was all about Me. She would talk to me the entire ride home. She would stop at the gas station and get me my favorite candy bar. (One that I didn't have to save for after dinner. I was allowed to eat it all, right on the spot.) We would stop for dinner at the local Holiday Inn where her sister worked as a waitress. She would parade me around all her friends, informing them of all my greatness with a beam of pride.

We would stay up late watching shows I wasn't allowed to watch, playing nail salon, share stories, and at the end of the night I cuddled up to her to fall asleep.

I would wake up to the smell of sizzling bacon and fresh biscuits filling the air. (Seriously the BEST way to wake up.) She would let me eat when I wanted, whatever I wanted. Some would say I was spoiled. She would never say that. She would say, "She deserves to have what she wants."

Grandma Hazel's Wisdom: We deserve to have everything we want. It is our birthright. It doesn't have to be earned, it's a given. We deserve to be treated as if the world revolves around us. We are entitled, because we are born. The fear is that we will create monsters. The truth is we will feed the soul the love it desires. We will be a source of love, acknowledgement, validation, and inspiration. We will reinforce and remind them of the miracle of their birth on this planet. We will create memories for them to reference when they forget.

I would help her around the farm all weekend. She always had at least 12 to 15 dogs at any given time. They required so much attention and care, and actually I was happy to help. We would look through the rooms in her house to find "treasures" and often I would come home with a suitcase of miscellaneous items I just had to have. She never said "no." When I was with Grandma Hazel, it was always a Yes.

Grandma Hazel's Wisdom: Yes is a lot more fun than no.

My Grandma's idea of a good time was going to Neiman Marcus or Saks Fifth Avenue, having brunch in their elegant restaurant, and ending the day shopping. Forever.

One Saturday, I was staying at the farm and my grandma invited my mother to meet us at Saks Fifth Avenue for lunch. We had a lovely lunch with tea and cookies (and a big fat bill). As we were walking out, a rack of beautiful rabbit fur coats rolled by, right in front of us. (Keep in mind this was in the 70's before fur was bad.)

Everyone, well at least the "cool" kids, had a rabbit fur coat.

The coats were often all brown, or multicolored, sometimes black, but rarely white.

The coat that rolled by caught my eye and I couldn't let it go. I screamed, "GRANDMA!!! Look at that fur coat." It was gorgeous, all white with tan panels about three inches wide running vertically across the coat's exterior.

My grandma immediately stopped the sales clerk and pulled the coat off the rack. I put it on and it was a perfect fit. My mother immediately looked at the tag and said, "Oh … my… God! You have got to be kidding me. This coat is $320." Her instant response was, "Take that coat off right now young lady, right now."

My grandma simply looked at the clerk and said, "We will take it." I almost lost my mind! I was in complete shock. She said, "If she wants a fur coat, she gets the best fur coat available." That was one of the only times I witnessed my mom yelling at my Grandma.

In typical Southern fashion, my Grandma calmly responded, "It's my money and I can do whatever I want with it. This is what I want to buy. You are getting a little big for your britches young lady."

And just like that, it was done. The coat was mine. (My

mom had her own way of making it right by only allowing me to wear it on special occasions, which, as you can imagine, rarely came about. I actually grew out of it before I had the chance to wear it out.)

Grandma Hazel's Wisdom: It wasn't about the fur coat. It was about wanting something and having no idea how you are going to get it. It's about believing in the possibilities you have no idea exist. It's about being open to letting things show up for you unexpectedly, a complete surprise. That's the real fun in life, all the surprises! There are so many surprises waiting for you to dare to believe. Believe. It's fun.

Grandma Hazel was always on my side. Cheering me on. Believing in me. Seeing my greatness. Always.

One Christmas, she came to our house to celebrate the day. She always had more gifts than anyone else to give. Her love language was definitely giving gifts. I was so thankful. Her gifts were always perfect. Exactly what I wanted. This year in particular I got a Huffy 10-speed bike from Santa. I had to ride it. It was so cold and damp outside, but that didn't matter.

By the end of the day, I was not feeling so well. I put my head down on the couch and fell asleep. As my Grandma

Hazel was leaving, my mom said, "Heather get up and give your Grandma a kiss goodbye." I was so weak and lethargic. I could barely lift my head. I said, "Mom, I can't get up, it hurts." My mother wasn't having that. At all. She raised her voice and tone, "Heather Reneé, get up right now!"

My grandma immediately looked at me and said, "You stay right there darling, I will come to you." My mother was not happy, not in the least bit. My grandma whispered in my ear, "Sweetheart, feel better. Merry Christmas. I love you so much." She kissed me on the forehead and headed to the door. She told my mom, "You better check her temperature. She feels really warm." And off she went.

I was sick. Very sick. I had strep throat that turned into a terrible virus in my body that left me on the couch for two weeks.

Grandma Hazel's Wisdom: When we are safe in our own love, we don't need others to behave in a particular way in order to make us feel good. When you can experience the love for how it feels, not how it looks, that's when doors will open for you. Rely on the feeling your heart has every time you see your special loved ones. That's all you need.

We had a special something together. She had two other grandchildren from my mother's sister, but they were never really interested in spending time with my Grandma. They didn't like the farm and avoided going down to visit.

That being said, I still feel like our bond was like no other. She looked at me with eyes of love. She listened to me as if there was nobody else in the world speaking. She reminded me, always, that I deserved only the best, in so many more ways than material objects. She was present. Engaged. In awe of me. I felt it. I knew it. She never said "no." She didn't have to. The world was mine and she was going to support me in all the "yeses" of the world. She was always about the possibilities.

Grandma Hazel's Wisdom: You deserve the best because you are the best. You deserve love because you are love. You deserve to be put on a pedestal to illuminate the world. You deserve to be celebrated in all your greatness. Humble pie is for the birds.

I was fifteen when my parents divorced. I chose to stop talking to my mother for almost a year. (I'll tell you all about it in the "Mom" chapter.) My mother was devastated and begged my Grandma to intervene. I received so many phone calls from family, friends and relatives to convince me to talk to my mother. I was mad. I was hurt. I didn't want to talk to her. End of story.

My grandma called me. She said, "Sweetheart, I know it's hard. I know you are hurting. You take your time. Feel it. Sit with it. Take as much time as you need to get through this. There are a few things I want you to remember. God doesn't give you anything you can't handle. Your mama will always love you and be there for you. Take as much time as you need. She will wait. And she will be there when you are ready. This too shall pass. You won't feel this way forever. Promise. This is not your fault. This has nothing to do with you. We all love you so much and want the best for you. Remember that. We ALL love you."

Grandma Hazel's Wisdom: Avoiding the pain creates more pain. It's not meant to be fixed. It's meant to be felt. It's meant to be honored. Given sacred space to heal. And yes, this too shall pass.

The years following my parents' divorce were some of the most challenging times in my life. I chose to live with my father until I graduated high school. I moved out when I was 17 years old. (I lied to get a lease on my own apartment.)

My Grandma knew I would never ask for help. She knew I was having a difficult time living on my own. I was working three low-paying jobs just to make my bills.

I would often get a card in the mail from her saying how

proud she was of me. She would always include a check, usually for $100, and in the memo line it always said, "Just because you are you." No other reason.

Grandma Hazel's Wisdom: We don't have to earn anything. What is given, is received, and given back to the entire world. You will never have the money you are worth. You are worth so much more than money can ever offer. Money is a tool. It only serves you when it's used as a tool, not a measuring stick.

Like my Papa Bill, my Grandma Hazel suffered from diabetes and kidney disease as she grew older. She was in and out of the hospital with poor circulation and eventually her big toe and part of her foot was amputated. There were too many hospital stays to count. At the time, I was living in Las Vegas and unable to fly back to Texas to be by her side.

There was one hospital stay in particular that felt very bad to me. I felt like I needed to be with her. Yet, I worried about whether I could get the time off work and, moreover, if I could afford to lose the income for the time I took off. Even so, there was a nagging feeling I couldn't shake, I needed to go see Grandma Hazel.

I literally said out loud, "God, give me a sign if I need to fly to Texas and be with Grandma Hazel."

Just then I pulled into a Burger King and right in front of me was a Texas license plate. Seconds after asking for a sign, there it was right in front of me. (This was the beginning of my love for license plates, there are so many cool stories coming.)

Grandma Hazel's Wisdom: We are giving you signs, all day, everyday. It's not a coincidence. They are there on purpose, guiding you to all your desires. Pay attention. Notice. Ask and we will answer. Always.

I flew down and went directly to the hospital. She was in serious need of a miracle. I walked in her room and she grinned from ear to ear. She said, "Hello darling, how are you?" I smiled and said, "I'm so tired, scoot over and let me lay down with you." Everyone thought I was kidding.

I wasn't.

So my Grandma slid over as far as she could in the bed and I climbed in. The nurses came in and said I was not allowed to be in the bed, I was not a patient. My Grandma simply replied, "I want her in the bed with me. It helps me feel better. She stays." And just like that, I stayed in the bed for the rest of the night.

Grandma Hazel's Wisdom: Rules are meant to be broken. You will know when and where. You will know what's right for you. Own it. The power comes in the knowing. When you decide what feels right, all rules dissolve ... in magical ways.

The diabetes took over her body. She was in pain, struggling more than any of us ever knew.

I was missing her. Sad for her. I wanted her to know that I loved her so much. I found a card that had a picture of a child on the planet Earth reaching for a star in the universe. It read, "Even if we are worlds apart, I will always love you." I felt a sense of urgency to get it in the mail. I wrote my love note, sent it out, and prayed for the best.

At the time, I was enrolled in a school for massage therapy. We had a huge project due that particular day. I was really sick and decided to stay home. I was on the couch watching a game show when I heard the garage door open. I looked up. My husband and my father were walking in. I knew something was wrong. I thought it was my mother. (She was battling health issues, as well.)

My dad looked at me and said, "Doodle, your Grandma Hazel died this morning." I ran to the bathroom and started throwing up. I couldn't stop. The pain was unbearable.

My card was on her bed, delivered the day before. Opened and read.

Grandma Hazel's Wisdom: You will never know how many people you have touched on this planet. Know a gift from God will drop in your lap and remind you. Cherish the moment. Believe your friend when they tell you how much you matter. Thank your parents for their unwavering love. Accept the praise from your boss. Know that the world has been gifted you. And you are loved "just because you are you."

We flew down to Texas immediately. I didn't sleep for three days. Literally... three days. (I now have so much empathy for those that suffer from insomnia.)

I could hear her. Whispering in my ear. Telling me all was well. Laughing at the ridiculous funeral arrangements. She was helping me cope. She was there for me, even when she wasn't physically there.

She continued to talk to me for the next few months. Eventually the conversations came slower and slower. And then she seemed gone.

Grandma Hazel's Wisdom: You get what you need in the moment. It's always changing, evolving, growing.

Sometimes we need to let go of those that have been holding us up along the way. There will be a perception of you standing on your own. But you are never on your own. We are always here, we actually encircle you, and any direction you choose to fall, we are there to help you up and get you started again. So the idea that you are doing anything on your own is simply not true. We are a collective force of love and light, helping each other light the way.

MOM

Mary Robie: The Head Cheerleader
My Mother

This has been by far the hardest chapter to write. While chronologically, my mom died 11 months after my Grandma Hazel, I didn't have it in me to write this chapter until the very end. It took me two days to gather the strength, a long pep talk from my godmother (Wendy), and too many tears to count. This chapter was the hardest chapter of my life to write, the death of my mom, Mary Robie.

I wanted to tell you all the wonderful things about her. I made the list.

How she was such an amazing friend. She would clear out our pantry to give all our food to her friend, her broke as a joke friend, with five kids and no money.

How she would go out of her way to bring seven dishes to a potluck, just in case someone didn't bring a dish.

How she would open our home to anyone that needed help, a place to stay, food to eat, a friend to listen.

How she was an amazing daughter, helping her mom at any given time. Supporting and loving her dad, especially in the last 18 months of his life, completely paralyzed.

How she would answer the phone at 3 a.m., get in her car, and go meet her friend that needed help.

How she would deliver food and presents to families in need on Thanksgiving and Christmas.

How she fed my cat liver for weeks to nurse him back from death. And when the vet told her to put my dog down, she let me build him a wheelchair out of a dolly and help him recover from a stroke.

How she put up with my dad, until she couldn't anymore.

How she never gave up on me. Ever. She believed in me and never let me stop believing in myself.

I wanted to say all those things, but I couldn't. I was mad.

Mad that she left. Mad that she left me. It's an indescribable pain. A pain I'm not sure I will ever recover from. It's with me. Every minute. Every day. I get so busy in life that it distracts me, but when I'm quiet, it creeps back. It sets in. And in an instant, I feel like my mom left me. Again. And again.

She said she would always be here for me. And she left.

I had plans. She was supposed to be there to be the most awesome Grandma. She left.

She was supposed to see me write my books and build businesses. She left.

She was supposed to be going to craft fairs with me, and carry the tradition on with my son. She left.

She was supposed to be here for me to call her when I had no idea what to do, how to do it, and when to do it. She left.

We were supposed to laugh together more, eat together more, and celebrate together. There was so much more to do. She left.

I miss her so much. And while I know she is around me in spirit, I miss her touch. I miss her hugs. I miss her holding my hand. I miss her laugh. I miss our time together. She was my best friend.

She is my best friend.

From the day she found out I was coming into her life, she knew I was a miracle from God. She knew there was a profound reason I was born and she made a promise to herself to always hold me in that space. Greatness.

Mary's Wisdom: The people in our lives are there by design. They are there to remind us of love. Love for yourself and love for each other. The reminders come in a lot of ways. Some are challenging and unpleasant. Some are easy and effortless. Regardless of how they show up, we are here to remind each other of greatness.

She let me be Me.

When I wanted to cook macaroni and cheese on the hot stove at four years old, she said yes. She showed me how to boil the noodles, how to drain them, and add in all the ingredients. She told me the box didn't give us enough cheese, so we had to add a half a block of cheese in at the end to make it good. She trusted me. She believed in me. She knew I was capable if I had the understanding I needed to complete the task.

When I wanted a drink, she let me climb the counters to grab a cup. She let me go to the fridge and get the juice out, open the bottle, and pour my own. And if I spilled, she said, "Don't worry, it happens to me all the time. Just get a paper towel and clean it up." Mistakes were not handled with a punishment. There was an explanation and a solution.

When I opened a business, like her, at five years old, she gave me old checks and deposit slips to pretend I was legit. She encouraged me in every way she could.

When I told her I wanted to make a gingerbread house for my Papa Bill on Christmas, she went to the store at 10 p.m. and bought everything we needed. We stayed up till 4 a.m. building the gingerbread house. (We couldn't get the frosting right. It wouldn't stick to the graham crackers!) We finally finished, got a couple of hours of sleep, and headed to my Papa Bill's house in the morning. I was holding the house on my lap and fell asleep. My dad went over a railroad track and the house fell into pieces on the floorboard of the car. I was hysterical. So sad. So mad. She helped me pick up the pieces and said, "It's ok sweetheart. Your grandpa will love it. I promise. And we will just get to eat it right away. It's okay my love." She could have been so angry. She chose love.

When I would get so pissed at her as a pre-teen, I would

go in my room and bend the wire hangers in anger and throw them across the room. She would come in my room, see all the hangers and ask me why I was mad at her. She knew I needed to vent. She knew I needed an outlet. And wire hangers gave me the revenge and expression I needed to get the anger out of me. She would say, "Are you ready to talk about it, or do you need more hangers?" (Eventually she replaced my hangers with plastic because they were harder to break and lasted longer.)

When I told her I wanted to run away, she would say, "I can help you pack. What suitcase do you want to use?" She knew. She knew I needed the space and freedom to be me.

When I wanted to rent a limo for my 8th grade dance, she asked me how I was going to raise the money. I was babysitting any kid, any time, to make the money I needed. When I told her I had the money, she set it up and cheered me on. She always encouraged me to figure out a way to make my dreams come true. If I needed help, she was there, right by my side.

Mary's Wisdom: We are here to cheer each other on along the way. We need to stand on the sidelines, stay focused on the person in need of support, and see their greatness, especially when they can't. We are not here to play the game for them. We are not here to tell them how to play the game. We are here to remind them to get back up when they fall, get back in the game when they feel like quitting, and love themselves enough to know when it's time to quit.

I knew she needed the same from me. I knew she was challenged with her own issues in life and I knew she needed to vent that out, too. I gave her the space to do it.

She would get completely overwhelmed with all the responsibilities of motherhood, being a wife, a caretaker to her own parents, a friend, household duties, and working outside of the home. (I understand this so clearly now, going through it myself.)

She was feisty. Short-tempered. Her buttons were lit up and easy to push.

When I caught her off guard with a smart-ass remark, or back talk, or sass, she would let me know right away that shit was not going to fly.

She would give me a look, or a slap, or a pinch under the arm (the super tender part that hurts like no other pain). And sometimes all she had to say was, "Heather Reneé" and the party was over.

She would threaten me with the "white belt," but she only used it one time. I completely embarrassed her when I was in Girl Scouts, technically Brownies. I never made it to Girl Scouts because I was kicked out for stealing. I stole another girl's wallet and it was in front of the entire troop and their mothers. She was mortified. The whole way home she never said a word. She told me to get the belt and she whooped my butt. She didn't feel good doing it, but she felt it was necessary. Truth be told, the belt had nothing to do with my regret. I was really sorry to put my mom in that position. She didn't deserve it.

She was so overwhelmed one night. After dinner she was doing the dishes and was so pissed that my dad and I were not helping her. She literally started yelling and screaming, "That's okay, I will do the dishes myself!" And she proceeded to throw all our plates on the floor and watch them shatter into a thousand pieces. She kept going, about five dishes in, my dad said, "That's enough!" and made her stop. She walked out of the kitchen and went to her room for the night. Shattered dishes everywhere.

The kitchen was her battleground. I think by the time dinner rolled around she was so exhausted she couldn't muster up the energy to keep it all together. One night we were complaining about her making spaghetti. She was tired of hearing it and screamed, "If you don't want fucking spaghetti, then fine! Nobody will eat spaghetti tonight." She threw the spaghetti sauce off the stove against the back wall. The sauce was everywhere, on the fridge, on our pantry, on the walls, and on the ceiling. (When we moved from that house there was still spaghetti stains on the ceiling.) She walked out of the kitchen, went to her room, and declared dinner as officially cancelled for the night. She said, "You're on your own!"

She was so ridiculously unorganized. When company was scheduled to come over she would do what she called a "clean sweep." She would take an empty box and go through the house loading it up with mail, scissors, food, and anything that was out and needed to be put away.

Then she would shove it in the garage to "go through" later. Needless to say, the boxes were rarely sorted through. She would ask me to go find the scissors and I can remember thinking is, "Where am I even supposed to start looking? Who knows were they are? They are in some box in the garage. Good luck!"

Mary's Wisdom: Our actions and behaviors are not a direct reflection of who we are. When we act out, that is just a symptom of the issue that is deep within. It's not a judge of our character. Have the courage to be unapologetically you. It inspires others to do the same.

Shattered plates aside, we loved each other dearly. A love like no other. We accepted each other. We honored the moments of anger and frustration. Sometimes we handled it with empathy and grace. Sometimes we expressed it in ways we wish we could take back.

Regardless of our actions, there was always love present. We both knew it. Our love was unquestionable.

She would come in my room every morning to wake me up for school. I hated rolling out of bed, especially early in the morning. (I actually still hate it.) She would start picking at my face, swearing there were black heads and pimples on my face that she needed to pop. I never had any acne or even the slightest blemish on my face. She knew that's what would get me out of bed.

Her routine was to make me hot chocolate and breakfast. Every morning. She knew that would ease the pain of early mornings and get me out of bed, too.

When I was sick, she would make me a special bed on the couch. She would make me the center of her world. Get me everything I needed. She would stay with me until I was well.

When I was constipated, which was often, she would come

and sit on the edge of the bathtub and hold my hand while I sat on the toilet. Dedication. Serious dedication.

When I was bullied and teased at school, she would make the effort to come to my room every night and tell me they were wrong. That I was here on purpose and they were wrong. She would promise me we would go on a diet together the next Monday. And then she would say, "Let's go make some cookies, that will help us feel better." And it did make me feel better.

When I felt ignored or undervalued by my father, she would make up the difference. She invested everything in me. I was her priority. I was her number one.

Mary's Wisdom: We are here as a collective force of love for each other. To support each other by holding hands, and often, holding each other's heart.

One day she decided she was done. Done with my father. While I'm sure it didn't happen overnight, as a young teen, it felt like it.

My father was not attentive, engaged, or even all that interested in living an exciting life in my years growing up. He was content to go to work, come home, eat dinner, watch tv, and go to bed. On the weekends, he would go play poker and repeat the usual weekly routine. Him and my mom led independent lives. They were friends, good friends, but certainly not lovers. Time and distance created a void that couldn't be filled.

I remember coming home one night from karate practice. She ordered pizza to be delivered to our house. She paid for the pizza, looked at me and said, "Don't get used to this. When I leave your dad we won't have the money to order pizza for awhile."

I was in shock. Complete disbelief. She "forgot" to tell me her plans. I was so angry. I was so mad at her. I ate my dinner and immediately felt the urge to vomit.

The next day she told my dad she was getting a hotel room for the next week to "think about what she wanted." She never came home. She left. She sent movers for our things. I said "No." I wasn't going with her.

She was shocked. Complete disbelief. It never occurred to her that I would stay with my dad. She automatically assumed I would go with her. I didn't. I couldn't.

My dad was devastated. He didn't get it. They had lived disconnected and disengaged for so long, he had no idea anything was even wrong.

The first time I ever witnessed my father cry was the day my mom sent the movers to our house. He was standing against the wall, sobbing hysterically. I walked over to him and he grabbed me, and fell into my arms. He was completely helpless in the moment. It was a cry I never wanted to hear from my father. He looked me in the eyes and pleaded with me, "Please don't leave me. I don't know what I would do without you. Please, please just don't leave me too."

She left.

I stayed with my dad.

I stayed mad at my mom and didn't speak to her for over a year.

She was devastated. I'm pretty sure I was punishing her in some subconscious way. I was so angry with her. I couldn't see her face or hear her voice without being disgusted.

She had family members call to persuade me to talk to her. She had family friends call to guilt me into talking to her. She had my friends call to beg me to talk to her. I was too hurt. I was so angry that she gave up on my dad and our family.

Mary's Wisdom: Our biggest growth often comes from our most challenging times. The challenges that show up are there to help us reconnect with the wisdom and love within. To remind you that you are worthy. You have the power.

She never gave up on me. For over a year she called. She wrote. She sent gifts. She did everything she could to get me back. She didn't know if I would ever forgive her, but she never gave up hope that I would eventually come back around. I was her world, and without me in it she was completely lost.

I held strong for over a year. But I missed my mom. I missed her love. It's a love that no one can replace or replicate.

Over time, I started to let her in. I would meet her for lunch. We would go shopping. Eventually, I visited her apartment. I started to accept that this was how my life was going to look. Divorced parents. Broken home.

I stayed with my dad for the next couple of years. They divorced when I was 15 years old and I moved out of my father's apartment when I was 17. I knew he needed me. I needed him too. I needed to build a relationship with him outside of my mother. We needed to get to know each other without my mom's influence.

Mary's Wisdom: Healing takes place when you least expect it. Sometimes life requires a challenging event to ignite your desired healing. We are not aware of the bigger picture, but it will reveal itself. Often that's when you feel tremendous gratitude for the experience.

After living with my dad, on our own, for a couple of years, I started to understand why my mom left. He wasn't enough for her. She didn't want to live her life watching tv and staying inside on a beautiful day. She wanted to go dancing, listen to live music, go on vacations, and live life. My dad was completely content to sit on the couch and watch life through a big screen.

I grew empathy, compassion, and an understanding for my mom and the decisions she made. I wish she would have discussed it with me so I understood where she was coming from, but that wasn't how it was meant to play out.

Mary's Wisdom: From the sidelines we can see another perspective. We can appreciate the situation for what it is, growth. Expansion. A return to love.

My mom started dating a guy that was the complete opposite from my dad, in all the worst ways. He was an abusive alcoholic, drug addict, and extremely manipulative with my mother. He was what she thought she wanted, until she really got to know him.

One night, my dad got a phone call and rushed out of the house. He said a friend was in trouble and needed his help. That "friend" was my mom. Her boyfriend had thrown her against the wall and hit her. She called my dad and he picked her up, got her a hotel room for the night so she didn't have to go back to her apartment, gave her money for food, and stayed with her until she calmed down enough to go to sleep.

They loved each other. They just couldn't live with each other anymore.

Mary's Wisdom: We hold a space in our hearts for each other, even when we are no longer together. The memories, moments, and love are forever stored in a safe place. It feels good to hold the love.

My dad never told me about that night. Years later, I was angry with my dad and my mom told me the story of the night my father helped her. She said, "Your dad is a good man. A very good man."

After I started driving, I spent a lot of time with my mom. I would go to her office and sit with her for hours, so long that we would go to dinner, too. I spent time with her on the weekends and would make time to be with her as much as possible. I missed her. I wanted to be with my mom.

I graduated high school, moved out on my own, and started my life as an "adult." I thought I was all grown up. I could handle my life on my own. Until life presented itself in a way that made me run back to my mama, crying, and wanting her to hold me and make it all better.

I was engaged at 20 years old and my fiancé decided to cheat on me. It was the only deal breaker I had. And he broke it. I was knocked down and couldn't get up.

I ran to my mom. She opened her door, cried with me, made me some cookies, and let me heal. I stayed at her house, in her bed, for two weeks. She never questioned me. She didn't try to fix me. She let me sit in the pain. Wallow in the pain. She brought food. She rubbed my back. She told me it was all going to work out.

Mary's Wisdom: We didn't come here to fix each other. There's nothing to fix. We came to hold each other's hand through the hard times, sit together in grief, celebrate together in joy, cry together in pain, and hold each other in love. We came here for each other.

My mom was right. Even the most devastating experience

in my life worked out for my highest good. One day I decided. It was enough. I was ready to start again. Ready to live a new life.

I don't know if she ever really knew the impact she made on me in those two weeks. She saved me. From myself. I was in self-destruct mode and she loved me through it.

Constantly reminding me it was okay to feel what I was feeling and it wouldn't last forever. She believed in me when I couldn't believe in anything. She knew I would recover with time and love. I did.

My life opened right up, just like she said it would.

Within a year, I was opening my pre-school and living my dream. She was a part of that dream in every way. She would come to my school after work and on the weekends to help me lay tile, replace bathroom fixtures and toilets, and paint. She was there to help me in any way, shape, or form. She supported my success every step of the way.

We spent a lot of time together over the next few years. Shopping, dining out, craft festivals, movies, and just hanging out. I loved spending time with her. She was always diving into new holistic ways of living. Reading self-help books, going to see the occasional psychic, exploring her spirituality, and learning about alternative healing methods.

Alternative healing had a history in our family. When I was about 10 years old, my mom decided to take a "hands on healing" class. The premise was that we have the ability use human touch to heal each other in so many ways.

When she came home to tell my dad and me, we laughed at her, made fun of her, shamed her, and told her "How stupid, Yeah right. We can touch each other and heal each other. Whatever. That's the dumbest thing we have ever heard!" The irony: 18 years later I became a certified Reiki Master and Teacher, (energy work very similar to hands on healing).

It completely shut her down. After she left my dad, she started to explore again. She started to take the time to see what she wanted to believe.

Mary's Wisdom: The people and circumstances in our lives are opening doors for us to walk through. The doors are leading us to our desires. If you can allow the circumstance to be the key to unlock the door, and see the people giving you the courage to walk through, the door will lead you home.

I was in karate for a couple of years in high school. I injured my wrist and had to go to the emergency room. The doctor said it would take at least six weeks to heal and I had to stay out of karate for the entirety. That wasn't an option. I had a major tournament coming up that I had to participate in. My mom gave me an option. She opened a door.

She was introduced to an amazing chiropractor who told me he would be able to help me heal faster. I rolled my eyes and said, "No way." Until the next day when I couldn't move my wrist. I didn't want to miss my tournament. I called her and asked her to make me an appointment.

That appointment changed the trajectory of my life.

I walked in, scared, not knowing what to expect. I had no idea how a chiropractor was going to heal my wrist. What I didn't know is that he was so much more than a chiropractor. He was trained in many alternative modalities.

I had no idea what he was saying most of the time. It was a completely different experience from a Western doctor. He connected the injury to emotional issues I was experiencing, did some corrective work on the injury and sent me on my way.

The next day I noticed a significant difference. Within a

week and a half, I was back in the dojo training with no pain.

Since then, he has been my primary physician. I have seen him for the past 25 years. I have experienced more healing than I can even begin to type. I will say that in my twenties I was diagnosed with HPV virus and underwent horrible pap smears where cancerous cells were discovered.

The Western doctors suggested I have a hysterectomy at 26 years old. I went to my chiropractor, had a session with him, and he warned me that I would be terribly sick for a couple of days. After about three days, I noticed the symptoms disappearing. When I went back to my gynecologist, there were no signs of HPV in my body, the cancerous cells were gone, and my pap smears were completely normal.

I have had so many beautiful, healing experiences because my mom had the courage to show me another way.

Mary's Wisdom: There are endless possibilities for healing. There are miracle workers on the planet waiting to help you in ways you didn't know existed. We are giving you hints and sending you guidance to help you find the light workers ready to assist you.

She continued to open the doors of spirituality for me.

When I sold my pre-school, I decided to enroll in massage therapy school. I was exhausted from running the pre-school for nearly a decade. After years of screaming, crying, laughing, and yelling, I wanted a career where I could be quiet. My mother was over-the-moon happy.

I was tired of being an entrepreneur. I wanted an easy job. A job where I could show up, perform a massage, and leave without a care in the world.

That lasted for 12 days. I was over it. Done being an employee.

I went to my mom and told her that I knew I could do this business with my eyes closed. It was an easy business compared to the pre-school. I didn't have the funds to start it. My mom did.

Mary's Wisdom: Help when you can. That's all. Help when you can.

She gave me ten thousand dollars to help fund the center and open the doors. It took some time to get all our ducks in a row. I decided to partner with a classmate and open the business together. We scouted property and applied for all our required licenses.

In the meantime, my mother's health was declining rapidly. A couple of years prior, she suffered a cardiac arrest episode in the park.

She was suffering from diabetes and heart disease for a number of years. We had her come live with my husband, Brian, and myself to help her "get on track." We vowed to exercise with her, take specialized supplements, and prepare healthy foods for her to eat.

One night we went to the local park together. Brian didn't join us on our walks together, but this particular night he did, thank God.

My mom and I were walking together and Brian was trailing behind us with our dogs.

My mom said she was struggling and needed to rest. I told her a bench was just a few steps ahead and we could rest there. She couldn't see the bench. She kept yelling that she couldn't see the bench. I pointed to the bench and she dropped to the ground.

Her face turned gray and her lips purple. She wasn't breathing. I was trained in CPR because I had been working with children for years. All the training was gone. I yelled, I cried, I actually slapped her across the face.

She was gone. She left.

I screamed for Brian. We called 911 but they weren't showing up. I begged to God, "Please tell me what to do!"

I heard an old woman's voice say, "Stick your fingers down her throat." I did it. She came back.

Mary's Wisdom: When you ask for guidance and get it, listen to it, act on it. It's there for you.

She was not coherent, but she was back. The ambulance was nowhere in sight, I knew the hospital was only five minutes from our house. I told Brian to get the truck. We were taking her to the hospital ourselves.

He drove the truck across the field to pick her up. We threw her in the back and made it to the hospital in minutes. The entire way I was begging her not to leave.

We pulled up to the ambulance entrance and got her in immediate care.

We found out she had suffered a cardiac arrest and was lucky to be alive. The doctor asked me if I did CPR. I told him, "No, I stuck my fingers down her throat." He asked me why I did that.

I told him an old lady's voice whispered in my ear to do it. He asked if this "old lady" was at the scene. I told him it was a voice from spirit, not in the physical.

He looked at me in disbelief. He said, "I'm not sure what to say, other than you saved your mom's life. When you stuck your fingers down her throat, you initiated a gag reflex that jump-started the heart. In the future it would be wise to not do this again. The masseter muscle that controls chewing in the body, can lock down on your fingers and sever them."

When my mom was stabilized and conscious, she told me that she saw her Grandmother standing by her side and talking to me. I let her know that her Grandmother was telling me how to save her life.

Mary's Wisdom: Our love for each other never dies. We are cheering you on, even when you can't see us.

She spent the next two weeks in the hospital. I left only three times to go home and take a shower. I couldn't leave her. The doctors suggested open-heart surgery, but she wouldn't consent. She knew at her core she would never make it out of surgery. She opted to test new therapies to regain heart function.

It didn't work. She was in congestive heart failure. Her health was declining rapidly. She was unable to walk more than a few feet, swollen from head to toe, and needed oxygen to breathe.

Mary's Wisdom: I was actually buying myself some time. Time to make sure my daughter was going to be okay. I just needed a little more time. The therapies offered me exactly what I needed. Time.

By this time I had opened my wellness center, Touch of Life, in November 2002. My mom was so excited to see the center open. She wanted to work at the front desk, but it was a hard sell for a wellness center when the receptionist was on oxygen.

When my partner and I went to the attorney to sign our partnership agreement for the wellness center, the attorney said, "You know what the fastest sinking ship is, right?" We laughed, a nervous laugh. He replied with,

"A partnership."

He was right.

She was not cut out to be an entrepreneur, at all. We opened November 11th and she wanted to take two weeks off for

Thanksgiving. I knew it would never work.

I consulted my mom and she said, "Just buy her out and get her off the business LLC." It wasn't that easy. She fought and bartered to get as much money out of me as possible. We came to an agreement and went back to the attorney, two months into our partnership.

I went to my mom's house before I met my partner at the attorney's office. We enjoyed lunch together that entire week. When I was at her house, I noticed it was a mess. I told her that I would come back over to help her clean up.

We had a very difficult conversation that day regarding her beloved cat, Mija. Mija was too difficult for my mom to take care of. Mija was the cat my mom got when she divorced my dad and I was not around. That cat got her through some of the toughest times and it broke her heart to let her go.

The only consolation was my dad agreed to take Mija for my mom. I knew my mom was struggling and begged my dad to take her cat. He resisted and would not agree. After pleading with him, for a couple of months, he consented.

My plan was to go to the attorney's office, sign the papers to dissolve the partnership, go back to the wellness center to work for a couple of hours, meet Brian at home, and then head over to my mom's house to get Mija to take to my father's house.

I told my mom what I planned and she agreed. Before I left she said, "If something should happen to me, look through everything for money. I have it hidden throughout the house. I have three thousand dollars in the fabric softener box, right here." She went in the laundry room and showed me a wad of cash in the box. I laughed and said, "Nothing is going to happen to you. Quit hiding money in places we would never think to look. You are so crazy!" We both had a chuckle.

My mom walked me out to her porch and waited for me to get in my Jeep. I started to drive off, looked over, and waved. She looked at me with an expression on her face I will never forget.

It made me sad. As I drove off, I couldn't shake it. I backed up and rolled down my window. She had a look that spoke volumes. It said, "I'm going to miss you so much Headie!" (That was her nickname for me.) I told her, "Mom, don't worry. It's all going to work out at the attorney's office. I will call you when it's done. I love you so much!"

She had a broom in her hand to sweep the porch. She held

on with one hand and waved with the other. The wave said the same thing, "I'm going to miss you."

Mary's Wisdom: Our souls know the story. Our eyes and ears don't want to see it. We both knew what was going to happen. We didn't want to say goodbye. We both knew the time was here.

After everything was signed, we were officially ex-partners. I called my mom immediately. There was a relief in her voice. She was glad I was on my own in business again.

I told her I was going to go back to work for a little bit and then I would be over to pick up Mija. She agreed and said, "I'm so proud of you my love. You are going to be fine."

Mary's Wisdom: We don't have to say much to each other to say everything we need to say.

I went back to the wellness center and my sister-in-law, Missy, had come in for a treatment. She had a terrible cold and wanted a "q-bath" detox that we provided at the center. She was with her girlfriend getting the treatment when I arrived at the center.

Missy was in the front room. I was standing in the doorway chatting with her. My employee, Kathy, was standing to the left of me next to the doorway. All of the sudden a giant, I mean GIANT, rush of air came through me from my feet through my head. My sister-in-law asked what happened. Kathy was standing beside me and felt the rush of air against her body.

We looked at the air vents and they were not in the right place to make that happen. None of us knew what it was. I joked and said, "You better hope that was a good spirit that went through me, because if it was bad, we are all in trouble."

Mary's Wisdom: I came through to say goodbye. To give you another reason to believe that I would never leave you. I would be with you in another way. A way that could be felt with the heart.

We all laughed it off as something weird. It wasn't unusual to experience unexplainable activities in the center.

It was later than I wanted to leave work, so I hurried out the door. I called my mom on the way home to let her know I was running late. She wasn't able to get to her phone fast so I wasn't too worried when she didn't answer. Once I got home, I called again. No answer. I called again. No answer. I called 10 more times. No answer. I knew something was wrong. I called Brian and told him I was going to go over to her house and make sure she was okay.

Brian insisted that I wait for him. He was about five minutes down the street and didn't want me to go over there alone. I was impatient. I called him back and told him I was leaving. He told me, "No, I will be there in one minute. Please do not go over there alone." I listened.

Mary's Wisdom: We are guiding you to work together. To help each other during the most challenging times.

He pulled up and we rushed over to her house. As we ran to the door, the silence was deafening. The dogs were quiet. Nothing.

We unlocked the door, ran inside, and looked downstairs. She wasn't there. I was yelling for her. No answer. The dogs were silent, cowering in the corner by the bathroom.

I went to run upstairs and Brian said, "No, let me go." I stayed back at the foot of the stairs. Begging God. Pleading for her to be okay.

Brian looked down the stairs, put his hand over his mouth, and shook his head from side to side. He said, "She's gone."

I screamed, ran up the stairs, and found her laying on the

bathroom floor with her head propped on the cat litter box. She was lifeless. We called 911 and they told me to do CPR. I started CPR and went to breathe in her mouth. When I blew a breath in her, it felt like an empty shell. The air just went completely through her body. There was no life. No spirit. No soul. Just a shell.

Mary's Wisdom: The body is a vessel for our spirit and soul. It is intended to be used and left behind. It's all temporary housing. We move on. And on. And on.

The dispatcher on the phone insisted on me continuing CPR. As I blew another breath, fluids came back out of my mom's mouth and filled my mouth. I ran downstairs, onto her porch and started vomiting. I couldn't stop. Neighbors showed up from all the noise.

A neighbor across the street was a fire fighter. He came over and confirmed she was gone.

She left.

The EMT's and ambulance finally arrived to pronounce my mother dead. The police came to investigate, confirming no foul play. The coroner came to sign the legal documents and release the body.

My dad came over immediately to be there with us emotionally and physically. As we were standing outside, the police officer came out and said, "Man, that cat is like a devil cat. She won't let any of us near her and she is just circling your mom, hissing, clawing and growling at all of us." I started laughing. I always called Mija a "devil cat" because she was so mean to everyone but my mom.

They wheeled my mom out of her home, in a black plastic bag. No words.

When we went back in, we gathered Mija and her belongings for my dad to take home. We picked up the dogs, turned off the lights, and went home. We listened to the song "Calling all Angels" from the Pay it Forward movie soundtrack. On repeat.

I held the dogs tight in my arms and prayed this was all a dream. I prayed I would wake up and it be back to normal.

I didn't sleep that night. It wasn't a dream. The sun came up and my mom was gone.

She left.

We flew her ashes back to Houston, Texas to be buried with my Grandma Hazel. When we had the services for my

Grandma, my mom bought a plot next to her. Little did we know that we would need that plot in less than 11 months.

We had a small service with a few friends and family. My mom's best friend from high school, Kathy, showed up. I was unable to contact her because I didn't have her phone number or information. When I asked her how she knew my mom was being buried today, she said, "Your mom came to me in a dream last night. She was running through the sunflower fields and told me how much she loved me, and said goodbye. I checked the obituaries this morning and found her name. I had to come."

I was so thankful she came and told me about her dream. It gave me comfort when I was in so much pain.

Mary's Wisdom: We show up in your dreams, in signs, in music as a constant reminder that we are never gone. We give you stories to tell each other so you remember the truth. We live on.

We flew back home to Las Vegas and returned to life. It never really felt okay for me. I was struggling everyday. I couldn't stop the tears, the pain, and the anger. She was only 52 years old. This was not supposed to happen.

Mary's Wisdom: It's exactly what was supposed to

happen. It was my choice. I took a little more time to die because I needed time to make sure you would have your wings to fly. I stayed to make sure you were okay. When I knew you were ready, I was ready to go.

One night, I was at the wellness center, sitting in a chair in the lobby by myself. It was about 6 p.m. and I was alone. Everyone went home for the day, but I was open until 9 p.m. so I stayed to accommodate a client if they walked in. It was quiet. I didn't do well in silence. I started crying. Missing my mom beyond words. The phone rang. I quickly went into business mode and answered the phone. The lady on the other line said, "I'm really not sure why I am calling …" I didn't even know what to say. She continued, "I have a coupon from this magazine for a discount on a massage. But I really don't even want a massage." I was confused and aggravated. Was this a joke?

She said, "Oh what the hell, can I come in and get a massage?" I asked her if she had a day in mind. She immediately answered, "No, right now."

I said, "Sure, I will see you in the next half hour."

She showed up and I had her get ready in the room for her massage. I got through the massage without crying, thankfully. At the end of the massage she said, "Can I ask you something?"

I said, "Sure." She said, "Sometimes I get intuitive hints and messages from the other side. Do you know a Mary?"

I lost it. I couldn't believe it. Was this a joke?

I said, "Yes, Mary is my mother. She passed away a couple of weeks ago."

She said, "Oh, now this makes sense. I didn't even want to get a massage. I actually don't even really like massages. I just felt this 'calling' to come here, and it had to be tonight."

She continued the conversation by telling me to thank Pat (my mom's friend who helped her accept her transition). And to thank my dad for taking the cat. She told me to say bye to Ray, my mom's friend. And most profound of all, she said, "Your mom sent me here to tell you that you are never alone. She is always here with you. She will move mountains to let you know she is here with you."

After a giant tear fest, we both left the center that night feeling a little closer to my mom, even though we knew she was so far away.

Mary's Wisdom: I found someone that was open. Open

to hearing my message and willing to help me get it to you in a way that wouldn't scare you or spook you. You needed to hear the message. You needed confirmation. You needed someone that was an "outsider" to bring you the message in a way that was undeniable. You needed proof. You asked for it. You received it.

Throughout the years I am reminded that she is by my side, more than I know.

She has carried on the license plate legacy. I see Texas license plates everyday, all day. And they usually show up at the most relevant and profound times.

I got mail addressed to my mom for over eight years. They were from different agencies requesting donations. They would send little trinkets, notepads, dream catchers, and even necklaces. One in particular was from the "Sacred Heart Catholic Church." My Papa Bill built a Sacred Heart Catholic School and Church. That was the first school I attended as a child. We made several moves and the mail always followed. No forwarding address request required. I still have a box of all the treasures she sent me.

Mary's Wisdom: We have the power to show up in mysterious ways. When you are open, we show up. When you ask, we show up.

She even visits her friend, Wendy, my Fairy Godmother, in spirit. She knew Wendy would be able to hear her, so she calls on her often.

When I was spinning out of control, feeling like I wanted to die, Wendy would call "out of the blue" and talk me off the ledge. She has helped me deal with the deaths in a beautiful way. Wendy has helped me cope and move through the pain, year after year. She truly is my Fairy Godmother.

Little did I know, until Wendy told me, that my mom would show up consistently and ask her to call me. My mom knew when I was on the edge and struggling. She knew Wendy would help.

My mom was a powerful force of love and light on this planet. And she continues to light the way from the other side.

When I sat down to write this chapter, I couldn't do it. I didn't have the strength or courage to step into the pain again. I called Wendy and said I couldn't do it. She simply said, "Write your story. If you are mad, then say you are mad." She gave me the permission to write from my heart, not my head.

I have cried more tears in this chapter than I have in the

past year. Wendy said it beautifully, "You tuck the pain in a corner and eventually you have to move it, over and over again. It never goes away, you just move it around."

This book has been such an amazing healing experience. I think I have actually found a place for the pain to sit. I can visit it, look at it, sit with it. But I don't have to move it any more. It has a home. It's safe. It's a relief.

Mary Robie is my mom. 13 years later, I miss her even more than the day she died. I have comfort knowing she is with me every step of the way. I pay attention, ask for signs, and thank her for being my mom. I'm so glad we chose each other. I wouldn't want it any other way.

Mary's Wisdom: We came together on this planet to make magic. To feel love beyond words. We chose each other, knowing that there would be so much happiness, so much pain, so much laughter, and so many tears. We knew how the story would play out, and we chose it anyway. There were times throughout your life that I left you. They were all on purpose. They gave you practice to fly. Sometimes you couldn't stay in the air, so I stayed to help you grow your wings. I left because I knew you could fly. And more importantly, I knew if I stayed, you would never soar. I had to leave, to let you fly. So keep flying my sweet Headie. I'm right beside you … the whole time.

OUR BABIES: HUMAN & FUR

Over the years, Brian and I were doing our best to create and grow our own little family. I thought I was going to have five kids by 30 years old. That didn't happen.

This chapter reflects our journey together, in the midst of everyone in my family passing away. My mother's side of the family left first, my dad's side is yet to come. Throughout all the deaths, we had hope. Here's where our journey began...

Brian and I met each other in what can only be described as divine intervention.

I decided, two weeks before I met Brian, I was going to let go of the idea of getting married and living a "normal" life.

I was done. Tired of searching for the guy who was going to complete me. Tired of dancing in the clubs, going on dates, being stood up, and really feeling unworthy. I was over it. I decided to buy my own home, adopt children, and run my pre-school. It was time to choose happiness. Choose my own life. Live the life I desired with or without a man.

I put a down payment on a townhome and started looking into adoption.

It was 4th of July and my friends were going to camp out at the lake for the weekend. I was thrilled to join in, feeling free and alive. I had a jet ski at the time, so we were having a great time enjoying the lake and all its beauty.

I woke up early and went out on the jet ski with my best friend, Stacey. We had a great time. The sun was shining and the lake was smooth as silk. All of the sudden, the jet ski died in the water. I couldn't get it to start. So we waited a few minutes to see if the engine was flooded.

A boat rushed by with three good looking guys, completely disregarding us. I couldn't believe they just drove past us without even checking on us. We were stranded. About 15 minutes passed by and they swung back around to check on us.

The jet ski had started again and we were ready to go. We told them, "No, we got this." I have to admit we had attitude. But we were still angry they didn't check on us before.

As soon as they pulled away, the jet ski stopped again. I couldn't believe it. I was so frustrated. They must have noticed we were not moving and they circled back again. The jet ski wouldn't start so they convinced us to let them tow us back to our camping spot. We arrived at the camp site, got the jet ski docked, said our "thank you's", and parted ways. (The three guys on the boat happened to be Brian, Keith (Brian's brother), and T.C. (his best friend).

The best part of the story: my jet ski started right up after they left and was running great for the rest of the weekend.

Two weeks go by and I decided to have Stacey come over for some girl time, shopping, and dinner. We went to Best Buy so I could get a stereo for my new house that was under construction. As we were coming out of Best Buy, a guy comes rolling up in his fancy car blasting his music. All we heard was, BOOM, BOOM, BOOM.

Stacey and I laughed, until he said, "Hey, didn't I tow your jet ski in on the lake?" I looked at her to answer. (I am the worst eyewitness in the world.) She immediately recognized him. It was Brian. We chatted in the parking lot for over an hour. I really thought he was interested in Stacey. (Especially because I had made my decision and I wasn't changing my mind. At least that's what I thought.)

I gave him my business card to keep in contact. I was strictly interested in the possibility of using his boat on the lake.

Two weeks later, he shows up at my pre-school asking me to go to lunch. We went to lunch and really enjoyed each other's company. He had just moved to town and I really thought he was looking for a friend. Nothing else. After we had lunch, we spent every night together for the rest of the week.

He invited me over to watch "Twister" on this new thing called a "DVD Player." (If that gives you any idea how many years young I am!) I fell asleep, as usual, and woke up with him next to me. I was running my hands through his hair. I didn't know what to do. If I stopped, he would wake up. If I kept doing it, my arm would fall off.

I decide to stop and take my chances. He woke up, smiled, and fell asleep. I woke up the next morning and he said, "I never want to sleep another night without you." It was beautiful, and we hadn't even kissed each other. This wasn't my plan. But I knew it was exactly what was planned. I knew.

Two weeks later we moved in together. And less than a year after he towed my jet ski in on Lake Mead, we were married.

We bought our first home and moved in on our honeymoon.

There was no doubt in my mind our universes collided in a beautiful way to make magic on this planet together. That, I know for sure.

As soon as we moved in together I knew what I wanted: a puppy. Brian was not as thrilled as I was to get a puppy, so he used it to his advantage. He said, "Ok, if you get a puppy, I get a big screen tv." I hesitated, to let him think he had the upper hand, and then I agreed. (For me it was actually a win-win: a puppy AND a tv!)

We went to the local pet store and found our Daisy Mae, a beautiful white and brown cocker spaniel. She was so adorable in every way. Until she peed, pooped, and chewed on everything in sight. She bonded with Brian immediately, of course. She was seriously the sweetest dog I have ever had.

We officially started our family. Our very first fur baby.

A few months after our wedding, on my birthday weekend, we found out we were pregnant with our first child. We were so thrilled to share the good news with everyone we knew. And we did.

I went to my first visit at the OB to get an ultrasound and check up. I was so excited to see our little nugget on the screen. As the doctor examined the ultrasound, the energy in the room shifted. She turned the machine off, looked up and said, "There's no heartbeat. I need you to get dressed and come to my office."

I couldn't get up. I couldn't move. *How did this happen? When you get pregnant, you have a baby. What do you mean there is no heartbeat?*

I got dressed and met her in her office. She told me our baby had died, I would miscarry the baby, and it would be as simple as passing a piece of raw hamburger meat. No big deal.

I left the office in complete shock and disbelief. I just knew she was wrong. I knew it was a mistake.

It wasn't.

It was Christmas Eve, 1998, when our precious baby left

my body. I was actually farther along than she calculated. It was not a piece of raw hamburger meat. It was a baby. I was in labor. I had no idea what was happening to my body. I felt like I was dying. Dying in every way possible.

I had to have emergency surgery on Christmas morning. As they wheeled me into the operating room the doctor told her team, "Let's get this done. My kids are at home waiting to open their presents."

I woke up in recovery, gathered my things, and went home. Grandma Hazel was in town. My mom and dad both came over, as well. We went through the motions, had dinner, opened presents, but I couldn't celebrate. I couldn't breathe. In an instant, everything changed.

We were devastated, yet hopeful.

A year and a half passed before we were pregnant again. This time, we were having twins! We were so excited and nervous all at once. I ditched the horrible OB I had before and found a new doctor from a friend's referral. This doctor was great. She knew our history and was dedicated to helping us bring our babies to this planet safe and sound.

We were flying to Houston, Texas to celebrate my mom's 50th birthday. She was so thrilled to have her 50th birthday fall in 2000. She thought it was good luck and planned for it years in advance. We decided to throw her a surprise party.

The night before we left, I started bleeding and having severe pains. I ran to the bathroom and prayed, begged, cried, "Please God, No!"

My doctor had given me her personal number to call if we had any problems. I called her immediately and explained the symptoms. She confirmed my worst nightmare. We were losing the babies. We were very early on in this pregnancy, so she said she would call in a prescription for me. She said, "Let nature take its course and know there will be another chance."

I didn't have the heart to cancel on my mom's big day. I went to the drug store at 10 p.m., got the prescription, and waited. We flew out the next morning. When we arrived, we let my mom know our situation. I slept on her couch for almost 12 hours straight. I went to the bathroom and knew they were gone. It happened again.

This time we lost two babies. It wasn't fair. It made no sense. *Why?* I asked over and over again. *Why? Was I not good enough? Was this my fault? Why was my body failing me again?*

Time. We needed time. The pain was too much.

We moved through life in constant pain. Our friend's were having healthy, happy babies. I wanted to be happy for them, but secretly I was so incredibly sad deep in my soul. I felt like I was broken from the inside out.

The questions kept coming. *Am I being punished? What did I do wrong? Why is my body not working? Am I not meant to be a mother?*

My world was falling apart.

A couple of years passed and then Grandma Hazel made her transition. When she passed away, she only had two of her many dogs left: Furby and Jill. (She had over 100 birds too.)

The dogs were hiding under the bed where my Grandma passed away. They didn't want to leave. They missed their mama.

My mom decided to take Furby and Jill home to live with her. My Grandma referred to her dogs as her babies. We couldn't give her babies away. We had to take them home.

It was a challenge for my mom to have the dogs. She was

suffering the complications of diabetes with major heart problems. My mother decided to move closer to us so we could help. She was in and out of the hospital and we knew her time was limited.

I warned Brian that I had to take my Grandma's dogs if something happened to my mom. The dogs were the last lineage to my maternal family. I loved the dogs. They carried the energy of my Grandma and my mom. I had to keep them.

We argued frequently about the dogs because we had two of our own. We brought home another cocker spaniel, Max, so Daisy would have a friend. Brian would constantly say, "We can't have four dogs." We agreed to disagree.

11 months after my Grandma Hazel died, my mom left this planet too. The dogs were cowering in the bathroom when we found my mom.

As the coroner walked out of my mom's home, Brian looked over at me and said, "Let's get the dogs and go home."

Furby and Jill helped me cope in so many ways. They reminded me of my Grandma and mom. They knew I needed their special love. They knew I was in so much pain. They would sit in my lap for hours and fill me up with love. They literally licked my tears away.

Shortly after we brought them home, Daisy fell ill. We took her to the veterinarian immediately. She was diagnosed with a rare form of cancer. This particular cancer made tumors multiply overnight. She was bleeding internally. Her stomach turned colors.

When we came home from dinner one night, the entire house was filled with blood. Our white tile was painted red. It looked like a crime scene. We rushed her to the vet and the doctor said her platelet count was 14,000. (Normal platelet count is around 400,000.) She was on borrowed time.

At the time, I owned the Wellness Center. We focused on massage therapy, acupuncture, alternative therapies, and an overall holistic approach to wellness.

We had a treatment where we used a bio-mat (a mat with jade stones and infrared heat) to help kill cancerous cells in the body. It was for overall health, too.

Brian asked me if we could put Daisy on the mat. There were no contraindications for animals on the mat that I knew of, so we gave it a shot. Brian had her on the mat for an hour. We didn't see immediate results, but we didn't give up hope.

I was sitting with Daisy and my intuition was kicking in full gear. Daisy was a healthy, happy, young dog. That was until my Grandma's dogs came to live with us. I knew. She was protecting Brian. Brian's mantra was, "We can't have four dogs." Daisy heard Brian. She was ready to leave the planet to make him happy.

I told Brian about my insight and we started talking to Daisy, telling her that we didn't want her to leave. We CAN have four dogs. We told her how much we loved her and how important she was in our family.

Her condition improved over the next few days. We continued to use the bio-mat and noticed her stomach getting better. We took her back to the doctor and she confirmed the cancer was gone. We told the doctor about the bio-mat, but she recorded it as a spontaneous remission, basically a miracle.

I didn't care how she recorded it. Daisy was alive and well.

It was a close call to death again, but we managed to escape it.

We felt so good.

So good especially because we found out we were pregnant. Twins again! I knew we were going to make it through this pregnancy. I felt it. We experienced a miracle with Daisy, I knew we were going to have another miracle in nine months.

Our other doctor retired, so we had to find a replacement. I went on another recommendation and hit the jackpot. She was an amazing doctor. Smart. Personable. Incredibly kind.

Brian joined me for the first ultrasound. I was so nervous, but had a good feeling!

I held my breath as she scanned my belly.

"There are the heartbeats!" she said.

Relief. Joy. Happiness. We were thankful. Incredibly thankful.

We went home to celebrate. I was tired and decided to take a little nap before we went out to dinner. I woke up, and went to the restroom. Blood. There was blood. I screamed for Brian.

He rushed me to the hospital. We signed in and they had us

wait our turn in the lobby. We waited for what seemed like an eternity. I ran back and forth to the bathroom, doing my best to hold it all together while I was miscarrying once again.

They wouldn't take me back to a room until I did a urine sample to prove I was pregnant. Absolutely ridiculous.

I went to the restroom to collect my sample and I lost the babies in the toilet. There are no words to describe the guilt I still carry. It was a feeling would never wish on another living soul.

After the nurse went into the restroom, they believed me. I was admitted to the ER and seen by a resident doctor. He told me he could do a procedure to make sure my body eliminated everything. I agreed.

I just wanted to go home.

I went home and something was wrong. I was hemorrhaging. I was in so much pain I started throwing up. I couldn't stop.

Brian rushed me to my primary OB. She said the doctor didn't get everything out and if she couldn't get my body to stop bleeding I would have to go to the hospital for emergency surgery, again.

I had a talk with my body in that moment. I said, "I know you are hurting, I know you are in pain, but I can't endure another surgery like this. Can we please let this doctor help us and let's just go home?"

My body complied. She did the procedure with success and I went home.

We were broken. Again. Hopeless. Again.

I called it. No more. I couldn't endure that pain anymore. It just wasn't in the cards. Not this time.

Years passed and I was going on a girl's cruise with lifelong friend, Stacy. I walked on the ship and realized that I really wanted to have a child. I didn't want to give up. I called Brian from the ship. I told him how I felt and asked him to think about it while I was gone.

I wanted to adopt. I wanted to make sure that's what he wanted, too. I got home. He looked at me and said, "Let's adopt!"

So our journey to parenthood took a detour, in a really beautiful way.

We were all in. Adoption agencies. Home visits. Financial Reports. Health Reports. Dog vaccinations. Everything was moving right along.

Thanksgiving weekend, we noticed Daisy had a little blood spot in her eye. By now, she was 14 years old. It was still unusual so we took her to the doctor right away. The cancer from 10 years ago was back.

They gave her some medicine, which we thought was for the pain. Instead, it was oral chemotherapy. Overnight, she went from a happy old dog to a dying dog.

I took her back to the vet in the morning and they said she didn't have long to live. The vet said, "Take her home, love on her, and let her rest." Brian decided to go to work after our morning visit.

We took Daisy home, put her on the couch with Furby and let her rest. I sat down to watch tv with her and she eliminated her bowels on the towel. I knew that was a bad sign.

Brian had just arrived at work, an hour away. I called him back home immediately. He jumped in the car and headed our way. I rushed Daisy back to the hospital and sat in the car with her.

I didn't want to go in because I knew they would want to euthanize her. I couldn't do it. Not because I don't believe in it, I just personally couldn't do it. It hurt too much.

I held her in the car as long as I could. I went back in the doctor's office and they took me to a room. The doctor said I needed to put her down, because she was suffering.

I didn't agree. She was dying. She wasn't crying. She was taking labored breaths, she was just going through the process. It was a painful process for me to watch.

The doctor said she was going to get the drug to put Daisy down.

She left the room. I looked at Daisy with so many tears in my eyes. I said, "Daisy Mae, I love you so much. I know you are leaving this planet. You have been such an amazing dog. We love you more than I can ever say in words. I have one last favor to ask you. Could you please leave before she gets back with that shot? I can't do it Daisy, I just can't. Can you please help me one last time? I love you so much baby girl."

The doorknob started to turn, Daisy let out a yelp, and left her body. The yelp was not a cry, it was more like a goodbye.

The doctor rushed in to give her the shot. I told her, "NO, she's gone."

The doctor didn't believe me. She checked her heart and confirmed she was gone. She was an amazing dog. She honored my needs, even taking her last breath.

When we moved out of state after Grandma Hazel and Mom died, we were only able to take Daisy and Furby with us. We found a home for Jill that had a special needs child that just lost her dog. Jill was a perfect match for her. We found a home with five children for Max to play with for the rest of his life. We missed them terribly, but knew they were destined for the homes we found. It was a perfect match.

Furby was all alone now, with Daisy gone.

Furby became the anchor to my sanity. We were going through so many ups and downs during the adoption process, Furby stayed by my side. To comfort me. Give constant love. Remind me that my family was there helping us along the way.

We were in the middle of the adoption and Furby started acting weird. He was drinking too much water, urinating frequently, and not eating. I was so fearful he was sick with diabetes or possibly something worse.

I scheduled an appointment at the doctor's for early the following morning. That night I talked to Furby. Actually, I cried hysterically to Furby. I begged him to stay until we got our son, Jacob home.

I told him, "I just can't handle another death right now. We are so close to bringing Jacob home. Can you please stay with me until we bring him home? I'm so sorry to be so selfish. I just can't bear to lose you right now."

The next morning I took him to the vet and they ran the entire panel of tests on Furby. The results came back.

She said, "This is the healthiest 14 year old dog we have ever seen. The only elevated level was his protein level, which is really no big deal." I asked her if it was possibly elevated because I fed him filet mignon. She laughed and said, "Yes, totally possible. Can I be your dog?"

I know he was sick. I know he healed himself to help me. He was there to take care of me in every way possible. I hugged and kissed him a little more that night. He loved me.

The adoption went through and our little boy was coming

home to live with our other "little boy."

Our Babies' Wisdom: There is a divine timing to everything. We knew it wasn't the right time to come, every time. It wasn't your fault. It wasn't because of your health, weight, or body. It was because it was not the right time for all involved. It's okay. It's really okay. We will see each other again, that is for sure. Giving birth to us was not just your decision to make. It was our decision together, and we contracted long before we were in these bodies how this was all going to go down. We are so sorry for your pain. We want you to know it actually helped you more than you know. It made you appreciate life a little more, appreciate the little souls on the planet a little more. It gave you the time and energy to take care of the family during their death process. It actually taught you to never give up on something you want. We reminded you that love could come in many ways. We knew Jacob had to be with you both, and if we would have come, he wouldn't be with you. Jacob is supposed to be with you. We had to carry out the contract. Jacob has amazing work to do, and we will be watching and cheering him on. We will all be together again. Promise.

Furby was getting older. He tolerated our Jacob, but the two of them were far from friends.

He was blind, deaf, and struggled to go to the bathroom outside. He slept for most of the day. But when he woke up, he would always come hang out with me for a few hours. He was old and slow, but he was still super healthy.

One morning I noticed he had a little cough. I was a bit concerned, so I watched him for the rest of the day. Brian was traveling for work, so I was alone with the boys for the week.

When Furby started coughing more, I rushed him to the doctor in the afternoon and she confirmed he was in congestive heart failure. His breathing was labored and the cough was growing stronger. She gave me some pain medicine and said a lot of dogs live with this condition for longer than you would think.

I knew. He was done.

I took him back home, made him some fresh chicken and hand fed him, crying, sobbing.

I put him on his favorite bed next to me and put my special blanket over him. I told him, "Thank you. Thank you for being the best dog ever. Thank you for helping me remember Grandma Hazel and Mom all these years. Thank you for staying with me when you wanted to go. Thank you for loving me for so long. You are simply the best."

He curled up and went to sleep. I woke up in the middle of the night and he was really struggling. I went to lay by his side. I heard him say to me, "Go back to bed. You don't want to see this. I love you and I want you to remember me as a happy dog."

I respected his wishes and went back to bed.

I jumped out of bed at 6:45 a.m. and looked over. I knew he was gone. I touched him. He wasn't cold, but he wasn't breathing. He was curled up in a ball, like he always slept, and his face was covered by his paw.

I was hysterical. I called a dear friend down the street, Natasha, and asked her to help. She came and took Jacob to pre-school for me and left me to take Furby to the vet.

I scooped him up, bed and all, and drove to the vet's office. She didn't open for another 10 minutes, so I sat in the truck with him, crying tears from all the death I had experienced over the past 12 years. Furby's death closed the grief chapter of my life. He was the last to leave of all my family.

The vet finally opened her door and I took him in. She

checked his heart and confirmed. She lifted his head and his eyes were open. I know that he purposely died the way he did to spare me the trauma of finding him any other way.

He knew what was best for me. He knew I had Jacob and I was okay. He stayed until he knew I was going to be okay. That love was like no other love I have felt.

Our Fur Babies' Wisdom: We were here to serve you. We came to this planet to be your strength when you felt weak. To give you love when you felt empty. To give you companionship when you felt lonely. To give you hope when all hope was lost. We were here for you. Only you. We are honored to be together on the journey and have loved every minute of it. The love was mutual, always. We are forever in spirit with you, curling up with you on the couch, greeting you at the door, sitting with you when you are all alone. We are here with you. Loving you. Always.

GRANDPA RALPH

Ralph Robie: Top Salesman
Paternal Grandfather

Ralph Robie was one of a kind. He was intelligent, opinionated, a professional photographer in World War II, top salesman for Sylvania, a pilot, and he was pretty confident he was right the majority of the time.

To me, he was just "the man that lives with Grandma Pat." Literally. I was in the grocery store with my mother, probably around three years old, and saw my Grandpa in the produce section. I blurted out, "Hey, that's the man that lives with Grandma Pat." My mother was mortified. According to my mother, he could care less.

I really don't have early memories of my Grandpa. My father and grandfather had a falling out and didn't speak to each other for years. My grandfather believed that my dad was wasting his life. My father was a hippie, free love, pot-smoking, poker player in the 70's and my grandfather was not impressed.

Grandpa Ralph bribed my father to attend college with the promise that if he graduated they would purchase any car he desired. (Dad was a car guy, so this was a big deal.) The promise of reward must have quickly lost its luster, because my father decided to become a newspaper distributor instead. My grandfather was disgusted. And so the feud began.

Grandpa Ralph's Wisdom: When we look at another person and expect them to behave or engage in a way to make us feel better, we never feel better. We always feel worse. We each have a wisdom that is guiding us on the path of life. The only soul privy to that information is your own. Mind your own. It all works out in the end. Everyone gets what they need from this experience we call life. Everyone.

My father went against my grandfather every step of the way. Including having a wedding without his parents' knowledge.

My Grandpa was incredibly disappointed in him and decided to continue that sentiment with me.

It started early. I was supposed to be a boy. In fact when I was born the doctor screamed out, "10 Pounds 4 ounces!" My father screamed, "We have a linebacker!" The doctor replied, "It's a girl!"

The joke was on them!

My Grandpa was hopeful for a boy because I was the last of the family tree. The "Robie Empire" must continue. I secretly prayed I would marry soon and drop the name forever. Just to spite them both. (That's what revenge looks like when you're eight years old.)

As time went on, I only remember going over to their house to visit on a few occasions. I have vivid memories from every visit because they were often humiliating and heartbreaking. I always left with the feeling that the life had been sucked right out of me. Leaving me empty. Worthless.

Grandpa Ralph's Wisdom: We have a powerful influence on each other, especially on our little souls. Choose your words wisely. When words are said from fear, they translate as darkness in the body. It's like a dark cloud comes out of your mouth and gets inhaled in your loved ones body. Too much darkness creates disease. Too much darkness creates depression. Too much darkness changes the spirit.

I wasn't used to that feeling. It made no sense to me as a child. My other grandparents were completely different. I was so confused and lost.

Why was I treated as a gift to the world by one side, and a menace to society by the other?

My grandfather decided to retire at 38 years old. He was home all day, everyday. Everyone worked, but him. He had nowhere to go and nothing to do. He was my emergency caretaker. Lucky me. I secretly prayed they'd never have to use him to take care of me.

My insecurities and feelings of inadequacy were reinforced on every visit. The commentary was consistent and relentless.

His criticism was never ending. When we pulled into their driveway I would start to breathe heavy in anticipation of the pain I would experience every time he reiterated, one way or another, that I wasn't enough.

Even though we didn't visit them often, it's amazing how devastating a few experiences can be. Just a few words on a few occasions had the power to change the trajectory of my life.

Grandpa Ralph's Wisdom: We choose the people in our lives to help us remember our greatness. Sometimes they show us rainbows and unicorns. Sometimes they show us the corn in our crap. It really doesn't matter how it comes. Often it takes someone telling us who they think we are, feeling awful, and igniting the inspiration to go inward to remember our own greatness.

One time when I was off from school for some obscure holiday, I had to stay at my Grandpa's house during the day. I was so excited to be able to watch my soap opera, Days of Our Lives. I turned it on and he looked at me, made a disgusted sound, and said, "You really watch this stuff?" I grinned and said, "Yep, it's a great show!"

He responded immediately with, "It figures. This is so ridiculous. You are losing brain cells by the minute watching this crap. Do you want to be this stupid? This is what you want in life? THIS is your destiny? You have got to be kidding me. Why don't you pick up a book and actually learn something. Would that be too hard for you? Forget college, just sit on your ass and do nothing all day." And it went on and on and on. So much that I just turned the tv off and went in my grandma's bedroom to sob.

I just wanted to watch a show. It wasn't my destiny. It was a show.

Another time, we were taking my father to the eye doctor and my grandfather had to drive us. My dad had severe diabetes and was losing his eyesight. I got in the car and my grandfather immediately took note of my attire. He scoffed and said, "Is that how you are going to the doctor's office?" I was completely thrown off and confused. I looked down at a nice shirt tucked into my "good jeans" and replied to him with a simple, "Yes." He smirked and said, "That figures. Entitled brat. So disrespectful. Who do you think you are? We are going to a doctor's office, not a dance. You should be in a dress to show respect. That's the problem, no respect."

I didn't say anything. I cried in the backseat the entire ride to the doctor's office. I cried in the lobby. I cried on the way home. I knew in my heart I was far from disrespectful. I was grateful to these doctors for saving my father's eyesight, which made the comments feel even worse.

Grandpa Ralph's Wisdom: When we look to a person of authority for approval, we will never get it or it will never be enough. Look for your own stamp of approval. Create one. Own it. Your stamp matters.

On the rare overnight stay, I would follow my grandma around the house like a little puppy dog. Grandpa Ralph was on better behavior with her around. On this particular night I was so hungry. (I limited what I would eat at their house for fear of judgment and a speech that would inevitably follow.)

I snuck out of my grandma's bed and tip toed into the kitchen. My grandparents were creatures of habit. They purchased the exact same foods over their entire lives. Wheat Thins. Diet Coke. Pimento Cheese. Morton's Frozen Cinnamon Buns. Oh yeah. My favorite.

I was allowed to have one bun in the morning for breakfast as a treat. Well, that night I decided I needed to have three buns. The box only had four buns in it. One bun was left. I didn't think it through. I just ate them.

My grandfather woke up to fix the buns. Buns … plural. He said, "What the hell happened to the buns?" I played dumb. He screamed to my grandma, "Patty!!!! Did you eat the cinnamon buns?" He already knew the answer. She didn't eat them.

I was sweating. Profusely. Praying that my grandma would say yes. Hoping she would "cover" for me. She had no idea what was going on and she simply said, "No Ralph, you know I don't eat those."

It wasn't the hardest puzzle to solve.

It was a mistake. A really big mistake.

He looked at me and started in. "What's wrong with you? Do you think that you are not fat enough? Do you think eating an entire box of cinnamon buns is going to help you? You are going to end up fat and sick like your mom and dad. Is that what you want? To be a disgusting fat pig? You want diabetes? You want to lose your eyesight like your father?"

That was the beginning. It lasted for way too long.

I sat there in silence. Tears rolling down my chubby cheeks. Fat roll hanging over my pants. Wondering *Why? Why did he hate me? What did I do? Why isn't he on my side?* Screaming inside my mind, *You are supposed to be on my team! You are supposed to love me.*

Cinnamon Buns. Cinnamon Buns. For the love of God. Cinnamon Buns.

Grandpa Ralph's Wisdom: When we attempt to control another by way of fear, shame, guilt, anger, we will never get the desired results. It doesn't work. This is proof. Compassion. Empathy. Connection. That's what works. The choice is always yours. All roads lead you home.

The comments weren't reserved for me. Unfortunately. They came full force at my mom, as well. And truth be told, it was painful to hear and watch him degrade my mom, but at the same time it was a relief for me to get a break from it.

One Easter, my mom invited all our family and a few friends over for a huge feast. She worked in the kitchen for hours to make a spread of food that spanned an eight-foot buffet table.

My mom's biggest pet peeve: food sitting on the table getting cold.

She gathered everyone together and said, "Everyone hurry up and get your food. I'm hungry!"

My Grandfather's response (in front of the entire gathering), "Well it doesn't look like you have missed many meals, now does it?"

My mother was devastated. Humiliated. Broken.

Hate filled my body when he came around. Sadness turned to anger. It didn't get better, it got worse.

My father had repeated conversations with my Grandpa Ralph. He advised him often to "Tone it down," or "Give

113

her a break."

Grandpa Ralph's Wisdom: Your problems can't be "fixed" by anyone other than yourself. We are not meant to "protect" each other, we are meant to empower each other. We are meant to give each other the support, wisdom, and courage to trust our wisdom. To act on our wisdom with the bravery we all have inside.

I was constantly on edge. Waiting for the next insult. The next declaration of my unworthiness. It's painful to anticipate it, to wait for it to happen.

Over the next few years he had a bout of isolation and depression. He actually did something productive and decided to join the Houston Zoo as a Docent. It helped him. He had value. He had responsibilities. He cared for and nurtured the animals. It helped. Probably more than I will ever know.

Grandpa Ralph's Wisdom: Nature has the power to show you another perspective. Nature, animals, the outdoors are all reminders of the possibilities and love that surround us every day. Everything is here for a reason, to help us in some way.

He started to be kinder. Smile more. Insult less.

It really didn't matter to me. He had hurt me for so long I had built a wall that wasn't coming down just because he bathed an elephant.

I was entering my teenage years. Painful. Exciting. Uncomfortable.

My father won a trip from his company to go to Jamaica for a seven-night stay in a luxury hotel. (My father was the cheapest man you will ever meet. He called himself "frugal," but he was just cheap.) My parents didn't go on extravagant vacations. This was a once in a lifetime chance. There was only one problem. Who was going to stay with me for a week?

You guessed it.

I begged, pleaded, threw temper tantrums, had mental breakdowns, threatened running away, and even gave my parents the silent treatment. Nothing worked. It was decided. He was going to stay with me the entire time. And there was nothing I could do about it.

Jamaica wins over me. Great.

He showed up at my doorstep with luggage in hand. My

parents jumped in the cab without hesitation. (At least it felt that way.)

It was a crazy week. The space shuttle "Challenger" exploded. A stray cat wandered up to our door and would wait for me to get on and off the bus everyday. Eventually I brought her in and used my parents' decision to leave me with a terrible man as leverage to keep the cat. It worked.

He was civil. I was civil. We both knew it was necessary, but definitely not preferred, to be together. It was necessary. To share space. To even talk to one another.

Grandpa Ralph's Wisdom: It takes time to heal broken relationships. Sometimes it just needs some space and air to breathe. It's not how it looks, it's how it feels. Be aware that the healing may happen long after you have left this body. It will happen. Time is irrelevant. Trust that it all works out, eventually.

After that visit, I realized I was growing up and rather tired of being fearful of his words. Tired of questioning myself and my worthiness. Tired of listening to his bullshit.

My grandma was set to retire. That's when they purchased a beautiful house on Lake Norfork in Mountain Home. That was the end of backup child care for me. I was so relieved and thankful they were gone.

Grandpa Ralph immediately went to the hospital in Mountain Home and applied to be a volunteer. When we went to visit the first time, we went to the hospital to see him in action. I was shocked. Everyone loved him. He was so appreciated, valued, and loved at the hospital.

Grandpa Ralph's Wisdom: We are our best when we are of service. Service looks different to everyone. Invest in yourself. Take the time to share the one and only "you" with this world. That's why you are here. To serve and be served. To give love and receive love. That's why you are here.

Everyone kept saying to me, "You are so lucky to have a Grandpa like Ralph. He's the best, isn't he?"

No words. I felt like I was in the twilight zone. *Really? Lucky to have this guy as my Grandpa?* All I could think was, "*What a bunch of suckers!*"

And then we spent more time with him. We went on train rides, explored the area, and we even enjoyed meals together. Something shifted in him. He was experiencing the beginning stages of Alzheimer's and Dementia. He wasn't himself. And quite frankly it was nice. Pleasant.

Grandpa Ralph's Wisdom: We have the power to change our mind at any given time. Sometimes those changes come with the help of a disease. The choice is yours. Always.

At the time, I owned my pre-school. I had uniforms for my employees featuring our logo in big print on bright, beautiful t-shirts. I brought my Grandpa a blue shirt and my Grandma a hot pink shirt. I knew neither one of them would wear it but it was the thought that counts.

My Grandpa Ralph rolled out of his room the morning after we gave them the shirts with the hot pink shirt on, tucked into his white and pink-striped pants. Really. He said, "This is great! The shirt matches my pants great. I love it!"

I took a picture because I never ... ever ... wanted to forget that moment. (This picture is included in the back of the book.)

Grandpa Ralph's Wisdom: When something good happens, hold tight to the love in the moment. Set the old stories down and create new ones. Now. The only thing you have to prove is love.

A few years passed and they made a trip down to visit us,

the last trip before they moved to Las Vegas permanently.

We met at Outback Steakhouse for dinner the night they arrived. My Grandpa Ralph had saved a spot for me right next to him. He was giddy. Happy. Kind. Completely uncharacteristic of him.

We had great conversations. He seemed to question everything. Like a young child. He even noticed a couple seated a few booths away. He pointed over to them and leaned in to whisper in my ear. He said, "Does that kind of thing happen here?" I had no idea what he was talking about. I asked him to repeat himself. He said, "You know, the Oreo couple." As I looked back I understood what he was saying. They were an interracial couple. I immediately replied, "That's not very nice, Grandpa Ralph." He immediately apologized and said, "I don't know what to call them." I replied, "We call them people, Grandpa Ralph. People." And with that, he got it. He chuckled and said, "You're right, people. Good for them. "

Grandpa Ralph's Wisdom: Sometimes our words don't match our intentions. Give each other the opportunity to clarify words to match their intention. We come from love, often we forget. Remind them of love.

I wanted to like this guy. I wanted to trust him. I wanted

to believe that the Alzheimer's made him forget he was a mean old man. I wanted to love this Grandpa Ralph.

As we were leaving we had to go to their car to get something out of the trunk. It was just the two of us. He opened the trunk and looked at me, right in the eyes, and said, "I'm really sorry I have been such an asshole to you for all these years. I'm really very sorry."

No words. Just tears.

Grandpa Ralph's Wisdom: Everything happens in the right time. Everything.

The diseases took over his body within a couple of years. It was time to bring them out to Las Vegas. My grandma needed help. It was time.

I searched for a home that specialized in care for Alzheimer's. I was losing hope for a decent facility. The "good ones" had a waiting list a mile long and a price that would bankrupt my grandma in a couple of years.

I prayed for help. I begged for an answer. I was given a referral to a great home literally two miles from where we lived. (It was also within seven minutes of my grandma's apartment I rented for her.)

I believe it was divine intervention. Unfortunately, someone had just passed away in the home, which opened a spot for us. I begged and pleaded with them to accept my Grandfather. The only stipulation was he had to be able to stand and walk on his own.

Once they were accepted in the facility, if they became wheelchair bound, that was okay. They just couldn't accept him in a wheelchair at admittance.

He complied. He walked for exactly one day. And he never walked again.

Grandpa Ralph's Wisdom: Help is always available to you. You just have to ask with clarity and purpose. We are all waiting to give you exactly what you need. You just have to ask.

His stay was not very long and he declined quickly. But we had a secret weapon.

Chocolate. He loved chocolate. And my grandma limited his intake on a daily basis.

I didn't. I didn't care. He had limited time on this planet. Give him the chocolate. So we did. We would go to visit, sometimes he would recognize us, most of the time he just knew we were in charge of "the goods."

The home had a huge great room for families to visit. Brian and I would sit in the middle with the bag of chocolates and wait for him to make his way over. Scooting his wheelchair with one foot.

He would roll up, look around with shifty eyes and whisper in my ear, "Did you bring the stuff?" I said, "Yep, it's right here." He would take the chocolate, hide it in his hands (melting it instantly), and roll off to the other side of the room.

He would make circles around the room, eventually ending back up in front of us. He would say, "When did you get here? Did you bring the stuff?" This would go on for five to seven rounds.

He was different. Funny. Kind. Thankful.

I could get used to this.

We got a phone call that he had fallen out of his wheelchair and was transported to the hospital. They ran some tests and found an extremely aggressive form of cancer. The doctors gave all the options and Grandma Pat chose to put him in hospice.

He wasn't in hospice long at all. The next phone call was from the doctor requesting a conference with the family. We knew that wasn't a good sign. When we arrived, they took us in "the room" (the one where they tell you the bad news).

Grandpa Ralph had stopped eating. The doctor told us this was a clear sign, specifically from Alzheimer's patients, of when they are ready to go.

Grandpa Ralph's Wisdom: We have choice. We can go fast or slow. It's always our choice. We often pick diseases, circumstances, or events that give us time to decide. We know when it's time.

He was right. Days went by.

One day I decided to stay in the room with him for most of the night. My grandma and my father were visiting him and I knew they needed support and love.

Grandpa Ralph was peaceful, quiet. He had stopped eating seven days prior and stopped drinking that morning.

I told my Grandma and father to go home. Get some rest. Both were struggling physically and emotionally.

I stayed. The nurse came in and put the blood pressure cuff on his arm. No pulse. She moved it to his leg. No pulse.

She looked at me and said, "He doesn't have much longer."

I didn't understand why he had no blood pressure in his legs and arms. I asked the nurse what was going on. She explained the body, in all its wisdom, begins to shut down blood supply to the extremities so it can preserve the internal organs. It was fascinating and devastating all at once.

She was right. He deteriorated quickly. He was no longer quiet. His breaths were labored and intermittent. He would stop breathing and I would think he was gone, then all of the sudden he would gasp for air. It was brutal to watch.

It was getting very late and I needed to get home. I knew I had to have a talk with him. I told him I was thankful for our time together and accepted his apology. I told him that I actually had a really good time with him at the end.

I made one final request. I asked him to leave his body before morning. I reminded him that he had already made his decision to leave. I begged him to exit his body before my grandma came back in the morning. I said, "If you love her, you won't let her see you this way. She left earlier with a peaceful, quiet picture of you in her head. Please don't ruin that for her. Please give her that peace."

He was unresponsive. But I knew he heard me. I could feel it.

Grandpa Ralph's Wisdom: We are always with you. We never leave. We can hear and feel everything. We are far from "unresponsive." This is the time when perhaps we are the most responsive.

I went home and two hours later, at 3 a.m., I got the call.

I made the call to my Grandma. We went and picked up her fragile self, took her to the hospice to say her final goodbyes.

We went in the room. He was peaceful. Quiet. I could feel his energy in there, holding her hand, kissing her forehead, whispering in her ear, "I'm okay Patty. I love you. I will miss you. I will see you soon."

Grandpa Ralph's Wisdom: If you are quiet enough, you can hear us. We are whispering in your ear. You may not "hear" it. You may sense it. Feel it. Smell it. Even see it. If you are quiet, you will know.

We left Grandpa Ralph's body that night, but we took his spirit with us forever.

I am so thankful for Alzheimer's.

Through its mysterious and joyful transformation of my Grandpa Ralph, I witnessed the return of love. No more fear. Just love.

Grandpa Ralph's Wisdom: Make no mistake. I chose this. All of this. I chose Alzheimer's so I would forget. I wanted to forget all the terrible things I had said and done. I wanted to remember who I really was. Without fear. Without judgment. Without regrets. I wanted to show you that I was love. Once you knew, I could go. There is so much purpose to all that we do. Believe it. Trust it. Know it. It all comes back to love. Always.

GRANDMA PAT

Patricia A. Robie: The Power Editor
Paternal Grandmother

Grandma Pat was the quiet type, not because she didn't have anything to say, she just waited for the most powerful moment to say it. And often, she said nothing at all.

Grandma Pat's Wisdom: There is power in silence.

She was a pioneer. Smart. Strong. Courageous. Decisive. Brilliant.

Grandma Pat worked for St. Joseph's Hospital in Houston, Texas as a medical editor for the doctors on staff. She was also noted in the press as the hospital spokesman and the Director of Information. She was so much more than I ever knew.

Back then it was a man's world, and she navigated it with grace and ease. I have a picture of her, (one of my all-time favorites in the back of the book) sitting at a conference table encircled by eight men; there were captains, corporals and Grandma Pat. You can feel the energy come through the picture. She knew her place was at that table. She was the only woman in the picture. She knew a seat was reserved with her name. She owned it.

Grandma Pat's Wisdom: You have a seat at the table. Any table you desire. It's not possible, it's already decided. It's reserved with your name. It might take some time to find your place card, but your seat is there, waiting for you. It is saved. The seat is yours, regardless of the time or location it is found. You deserve to be at the table. You will find it. You will see your name on it. You will own it.

To me, she was my Grandma Pat. A distant Grandma. Rarely gave a hug or kiss. Concerned about my grades rather than my feelings. Quiet. Good grief, she was quiet. Stoic. Didn't smile much or laugh often. The definition of an introvert. Always, I mean always, reading. The original cat lady. (She would breed and show cats as a side hobby.) She was actually the complete opposite of Grandma Hazel.

My parents felt extreme judgment from my grandparents. They were completely disappointed in my father's career and life choices. And voiced their disapproval often. They were in England when my parents married each other. It hurt my Grandma Pat so much and fueled the rage in my Grandpa Ralph.

It was a strain on their relationship and completely stalled the opportunity for me to build a relationship with them as my grandparents.

As I mentioned, they were the backup plan when my parents were out of people to ask to take care of me. I can count on one hand the number of overnight stays I had at their home.

Like my Grandpa Ralph, I struggled to have a relationship with my grandmother.

I mistook her silence as disapproval.

I assumed her head was buried in a book every time I stayed with her because she didn't like me or didn't want me there.

I perceived her concern for my education and grades as a constant measuring stick for my worthiness.

I interpreted her lack of affection as lack of love.

It was all miscommunication.

Grandma Pat's Wisdom: Our perceptions and assumptions often create a story in our mind that is not reflective of the story in our heart. We come from a great source of love. Look for the love in each other. That doesn't mean we all have to be friends. It simply means to honor the love that is present in every human soul. That's all.

But as a young child, my experience was a constant feeling of unworthiness, disappointment, disapproval, and an overall sense of feeling unloved.

I will say it wasn't all bad. There were moments. Moments when she let love in.

Every time I stayed at her house she would bring out the same book, "Sesame Street: Grover and the Everything in the Whole Wide World Museum." We would read that book for hours. At least it felt like hours. She would turn the page and describe every single item. She craved the written word. She wanted me to crave it too. I didn't.

As we would read the book, she would put a page in between her index finger and middle finger and run the page up and down. She would do it with sheets, paper, really anything she could get her hands on. Her left hand was constantly moving. It was a totally unconscious behavior, she was completely unaware of her little habit. I was completely unaware too.

Until … fast forward 30 years, she was in the hospital for what ended up being a quintuple bypass heart surgery at 75 years old. She is in her hospital bed, running her fingers through the sheets at record pace.

It never occurred to me that I got that habit from her. I, too, run my fingers through the blankets. I always thought it was because my hands were always hot and the cool touch of silk on a blanket would feel great, but it's actually a piece of my Grandma that lives in me. I smiled and had a chuckle when I was aware of how much she actually did influence me.

Grandma Pat's Wisdom: We are silently influencing each other in beautiful ways. We are picking up coping mechanisms, skills, and knowledge from each other along the way. You take a piece of those that you love (and often those that are hard to find the love for) and you save it for later, when you need it.

On one of the rare nights I was staying over, she called me into the bedroom to show me all her "special" treasures. She showed me a comb and mirror set that was her mother's.

(Her mother died when she was eight years old. Great-Grandma Ramona was also an editor for a newspaper, a woman editor in the early 1900's. Amazing.) She showed me her opal ring and promised it would be mine one day. We had the same birthstone, the opal. It mattered to her, more than I will probably ever know. She pulled out a gorgeous necklace from the California gold rush. And presented me with pearls that were her mother's. I remember that moment vividly. She let love out. She let love in. Our relationship had a healing in that moment. I felt loved. Valued. Honored.

Grandma Pat's Wisdom: Love shows up in so many ways. Love looks different. It feels different. It expresses different in each and every one of us on this planet. The fact still remains the same. Love is Love. When we recognize that, we begin to see it in everyone and everything. That's all.

As she aged, she grew softer. More compassionate. Caring. Less judgmental, more loving.

When they decided to move to Mountain Home, our visits together became few and far between.

They didn't come to my graduation. I was so angry. Especially because their entire focus was my education and getting the scores I needed to be successful in their eyes. I was hurt and disappointed. I wanted to witness their pride. It didn't happen.

Many years later I found out Grandma Pat was being awarded the distinguished position of President of the American Medical Writers Association. She was the first female President that did not have a college education. It was the same day as my graduation. She had worked for that position for more than two decades. I wish I would have known. (I actually have her framed gavel in my office as a reminder of what greatness looks like when the world tells you it's not possible.)

Grandma Pat's Wisdom: Things aren't always what they seem. When people behave or make a choice you disagree with, it's not always about you. In fact, it is rarely about you. We are meant to take care of self ... first. It's far from selfish. It's necessary. No need for apologies or excuses. That's a waste of time, and most often the biggest regret. This is your life. Your journey. Own it as your own. Grab your seat.

They didn't come to our wedding. Grandma Pat suffered a blocked carotid artery in her neck, resulting in a stroke. She suffered through a hip replacement at the same time. And while I understood she was in no shape to travel, I missed her there. I actually wanted her to see me in greatness.

To be proud of me. To love me. Selfish as it sounds, that's exactly how I felt.

We made an effort to visit them a couple of times in Arkansas after we were married. It was important to my dad, so we made the best of a situation that was often not so pleasant.

A few more years passed and we got the phone call. The one where my Grandma Pat relayed, "Your Grandpa put the remote control for the tv in the freezer and the ice cream on the end table."

Grandma Pat had this all under control. She had everything planned out for years. Finances. Directives for death. Everything planned. Even when Alzheimer's and Dementia entered our world.

Decisions had to be made.

She made the decision to move out to Las Vegas so we could help her with my grandfather and be close to my father and me. (We were our entire family. I was an only child. My father was an only child. My Grandma and grandpa were only children. Our entire family lineage stopped with me. I am the last branch on the tree.)

Grandma Pat's Wisdom: Too often we complicate things with emotions. Decisions are made and life goes on. Take time to be sad or disappointed with the circumstances and make a decision to set it down and move forward. Move forward knowing that this will all work out in your favor. It's just not necessary to get all worked up about something you can't change. Move forward. The choice is always yours.

We chartered a plane to get my grandfather safely to Las Vegas. As soon as they landed, he went straight to the care facility. She would visit him everyday. Sometimes he remembered her. Most of the time he didn't. She never gave up on him. Married 64 years. She never gave up.

Grandma Pat's Wisdom: Hold on to the people in your life that witness your greatness, sit with you in sadness, honor your wisdom, and understand your love. You were born to serve each other.

Being in the same town helped us mend and create a meaningful relationship. I was "grown up" and aware of the miscommunication that had occurred over the years.

I found her an apartment five minutes away from our home. She didn't want to live with anyone. She was fiercely independent. She didn't need anyone to "take care" of her.

She was clear how she would leave the planet. Fast and no suffering. As long as I can remember, she would say that she would decide when she is ready to leave. And under NO circumstances should you revive her. She was perfectly clear. NO resuscitation.

Grandma Pat's Wisdom: *This is your life. You get to make the rules.*

I was lucky to spend time with Grandma Pat. She was such a brilliant writer and a gifted artist. I grew to appreciate her in so many ways over the years she was living near us.

I was visiting her on an early afternoon. I mustered up the courage to ask her for a favor. A big favor. I was creating my first product to sell, WiseTalk for Families. It was a game I designed to help create meaningful communication and connection between parents and their children.

I asked her if she would be willing to edit the book that was included with the game. It was a big ask in so many ways. I was scared that she would say no. I was nervous. What if she read it and thought it was crap? I asked anyway. Her response was simple, "Well of course, dear."

Grandma Pat's Wisdom: *Sometimes a "favor" is a gift that is waiting to be given. It's waiting for the "ask."*

It took her a couple of weeks to review and edit. She never commented about the book when I would visit during those weeks. Nothing. I was so nervous. I had shared the most personal piece of me, my art, my creation.

She invited me over for dinner and gave me the book back. It was hand edited in red ink. My heart sank to my feet. My pulse was racing.

She looked at me and gave me a card. The card said "Congratulations. You did it." She added a special line to the card, "Thank you. I finally feel like I know you. I love you darling."

I was broken. More tears than I ever expected.

I finally felt the love I had craved for so many years. I felt heard. Acknowledged. Understood. Appreciated. Accepted. I felt a love for her I had never experienced with her.
It was a magical, meaningful moment I will never forget.

Something happened after she edited the book. She broke open.

She left a message on our answering machine that I still have 11 years later. She started with her normal requests, "Pick up diapers and chocolate for grandpa." But then her voice started to crack.

She said, "Thank you sweetheart for taking care of this for me. I love you and Brian so much. I am so sad I wasn't able to be there for your beautiful wedding. It broke my heart. I love you sweetheart, so much. I am so proud of you."

A gift I will never forget.

Grandma Pat's Wisdom: Love has to come out. It has to exit the body. It's meant to heal. It's not just your own healing, it's the collective healing of the world.

My grandfather passed away shortly after. She never really showed much emotion. She cried, but she would pull it all together to get all the practical details out of the way. We didn't have a funeral. He was just cremated and his ashes were stored on the shelf in her closet.

The next three years were lonely times for her. She continued on with her hobby in the study of our family genealogy. Life was so busy. We didn't visit as much as we should have. The guilt still lingers for me.

She never complained. Living on her own was beginning to take a toll. She was not able to drive or leave the house without help. She knew it was time. She was practical.

Unemotional. A home was the only answer.

And so we packed her up and moved her into assisted living. She would entertain friendships during lunch, but that was the extent of her socialization. She lived in her 9x14 room. It had everything she needed. Books. Wheat thins. Pimento Cheese. Whiskey. Lots of Books. And the cat.

I have never actually met anyone like her. She loved books, hated music. And as I recalled over time, they never had music playing in the car or the house. She said, "I don't hear what you people hear. It just sounds like terrible noise to me. I really dislike music."

Grandma Pat's Wisdom: You have the right to have an opinion. It's yours. And for those that disagree, good. Because they too have a right to their opinion. That's what makes the world go round. Opinions and preferences are forgotten, love remains.

The walls were coming down. I was actually beginning to understand and appreciate my Grandma Pat.

I was running my wellness center at the time. I was in the middle of a massage and my employee came to get me. (I knew it was important if they interrupted the massage.)

My Grandma was on the phone. I could barely understand her through the tears and cracking voice.

She said, "I need your help."

It was such a shock to me because she never asked for help. Never.

I said, "Of course, how can I help?"

Her cat of 18 years, Scooter, had suffered terrible seizures throughout the day. She needed to get her to a vet to be put down and relieve her of her suffering.

I told her I would be right there and immediately called Brian to help.

We went to her house and the cat was struggling to breathe. We rushed to the vet and as soon as we pulled in and parked the car, the cat took her last breath. We went in and my Grandma said her goodbyes. It was the first time I really experienced my Grandma grieving.

She said two words the entire ride home, "Thank you."

Grandma Pat's Wisdom: We are born to help. If you only knew how many people you have to help you at any given moment, you would never be scared again. You are allowing someone to share their wisdom, compassion, and love. When you have the courage to ask for help, you are inspiring cooperation and compassion around the world.

Shortly after her cat passed, my husband was offered a position with a company in Northern California. It was an opportunity that we couldn't pass up. We were hesitant to leave my father and Grandma. It was a painful and guilt-ridden decision, but ultimately we decided to move.

I didn't see my Grandma much after we moved. We only shared a few holidays together. I could tell she was lonely, and really bored.

She was over it.

I was in contact with my father often regarding her health and well- being. On this particular day, I decided to take the day off of work and treat myself to a massage from a fellow therapist in San Francisco.

I pulled into the parking space and turned off the car. I heard my Grandma Pat whisper in my ear, "I'm leaving now."

Grandma Pat's Wisdom: Listen to the whispers. They are real. They have meaning. They are there to help you along the way.

I thought it was just my imagination, but I called my dad to check in, just in case. When I called, I got his voicemail. That was pretty typical for my father, so I left a message and told him I was getting a massage and my phone would be off for the next hour and a half.

I couldn't shake the feeling that something was wrong. I went into the massage and did my best to relax.

As soon as I returned to my car, my phone had a voicemail message. It was my dad. He said, "Your grandma had cardiac arrest and died on the table in the ER. It took many attempts, but they revived her. We don't know what is going to happen next, she is unresponsive."

She explicitly said that she did not want to be resuscitated. She had her DNR in place 30 years ago. This is not what she wanted.

I immediately called and told him I would be on the next flight out. He said to wait until the morning when we would have more information. I hesitated, but honored his wishes.

I was grabbing dinner for Brian and myself and my phone rang. It was my dad. He was broken.

Sobbing so hard I couldn't understand him. He said that she had another major cardiac arrest and he told them to let her go.

I realized that a medical directive is easy to write, but hard to follow through on.

Grandma Pat's Wisdom: No amount of intervention can change a decision that has already been made. Make peace with the choices that your loved ones make. Our wish is not always their desire. The choice is their own, always.

I couldn't get it together to drive home. I had to sit in the parking lot until my eyes were capable of seeing the road. The only thought that circled my mind was, "I didn't thank her for the fruitcake! I didn't thank her for the fruitcake."

My birthday was a few weeks before my Grandma died. She sent me a fruitcake. When I got the package, I wasn't thankful. I was pissed. Who sends someone a fruitcake for their birthday? I hate fruitcake. How does she not know me??? Seriously... fruitcake.

Ungrateful. Selfish. Rude. Stubborn.

I got home, grabbed the fruitcake and sat with it. Crying, sobbing and repeating over and over again, "I didn't thank her for the fruitcake."

Grandma Pat's Wisdom: It's not about the fruitcake. And my love for you was never based on a "thank you." Truly. I whispered in your ear because I knew you would hear.

It was my final act of love to you. I spoke to you in a way you would understand and appreciate. I did it on purpose.

I knew I was going to die. I planned it until the doctors brought me back. I was not happy about that. At all. But I had a plan B. It was my time. I was ready. I will always be with you dear one. Always.

DAD

Alan Robie (aka: Big Al):
The Compassionate Soul
My Father

Alan Robie was a lover of life. He was simple, easy going, and one of the kindest people I have ever met on this planet. He was that guy, the one who didn't say anything bad about anyone. If he was thinking it, he didn't say it. His motto, "If you can't something nice, don't say anything at all." He lived it.

Al's Wisdom: It's not necessary to say the things that come in our mind. It's wise to run anything you want to say by your heart. Your heart will let you know if silence is a better option ... for all.

He loved fast cars, specifically, Corvettes. Lots of Corvettes. He owned 13 'vettes over his lifetime. When my parents found out I was coming into the world, there was a lot of financial stress in their marriage.

One month before my mom was scheduled to deliver me, my father went out and purchased the most practical vehicle, a Corvette. I was two weeks late so the doctors had my mom come up to the hospital to induce labor.

My father pulled up to the front door in the Corvette. My mom said, "Oh for God's sake, you have to be kidding me." My dad simply responded, "Oh come on, when will I ever get to go as fast as I want and not get a ticket?" So off he went, over a 100 miles an hour (at least that's my mom's memory of it), and they pulled up to the admission desk, rolling my mom out of the 'vette, 9 ½ months pregnant.

The hospital staff was appalled. My dad was grinning from ear to ear.

Al's Wisdom: Sometimes you just have to drive fast and know that the angels are guiding you along the way. Let the observers have their opinion. Stand in your joy anyway. This is your life. Your rules. Your time to shine.

My first car ride home was in the back coupe of the 'Vette. My mom was furious. My dad was ecstatic. He was so happy I was riding home in style.

He raced in the SCCA, Sports Car Club of America, along with my mother, for the majority of my childhood. He loved to go fast. He would take me on "a special ride" and go as fast as he could on all the back roads. He swears I would say, "Go faster daddy." But my memory was, "Slow down daddy." He loved the convertible top down, wind in his hair, sun on his face. He loved life.

Al's Wisdom: Our perceptions may be different, but the memory is the same. Love.

Big Al started playing poker in college and never quit. He loved gambling. He would frequent "poker night" more than my mother desired. He lost often, but when he won it was like Christmas. Microwaves. Diamond rings. He knew how to suck up to my mom so he could continue playing.

After he was laid off from his career as a newspaper distributor, he went to school and became a professional poker dealer for the Orleans Casino in Las Vegas. I always thought he would stop playing once he became a dealer. Nope. He would play on his days off. He loved the game.

Al's Wisdom: All paths lead to your greatest desire. Do what you love and the love will find you.

What I know for sure: I was the biggest love in his life. He adored the ground I walked on. He never raised his voice to me and had no desire to ever spank me. He was clear in his energy. I could feel his energy and that was enough for me. I knew when he was disappointed, hurt, angry, or sad. He would look me in the eyes and talk to my soul. No words necessary.

Al's Wisdom: We speak to each other with so much more than words. Words often get in the way of our heart. When we look each other in the eye and let our souls speak to each other, magical moments happen. We hear the truth.

When Brian and I got married, my dad prepared a speech to deliver at the end of the ceremony. He was so nervous. His voice was cracking. He began the speech with, "They say you can measure a man's worth by his accomplishments in life. I only have one, along with her mother, and she's standing right there. "

He continued on with all the greatness he witnessed in life with me and through me. Complete tearjerker. Brought everyone to tears. I will never forget the feeling of being loved by someone so much.

Al's Wisdom: When we have the courage to speak our own truth, we inspire others to connect to their truth and share it with the world. That's why we are here, to share our truth with the world. Stand up for what you believe in, even if you are standing alone.

Even though I had many magical moments as an adult, moments of feeling so much love from him, my childhood didn't feel so full of love all the time.

A big love for my father was television. I can't even explain how much tv this guy watched. He would sit at his desk to do "paperwork" and watch tv for the majority of the night. Most nights.

I was a human remote control for many years. Standing at the big console box in his office flipping channels until he found his show. Star Trek, Mash, The Honeymooners, I Love Lucy, oh, and the news, lots of news.

I would stand in front of the tv to get his attention and he would say, "You make a better door than a window. MOVE."

His love for tv never ended. He would get a new list of favorites each season and invest his time at his desk, eyes glued on the tube. As a child, it hurt. He was removed from our family. Unengaged. And really nothing felt worse than being replaced by a tv. (I think it's the equivalent of a phone for our generation.)

As time went on, I started to understand his obsession with television was really an escape. A way to numb out from life. To live life vicariously through his favorite characters. To escape the lingering feeling of failure. His father told him for years he was never enough. I think he believed him.

Al's Wisdom: We need to escape. It feels good to escape. Remember to come back. Come back to life. Come back to why you are here. What you can share. How you can serve. We are meant to be here. It's okay to leave, just come back to play in the game. You are an important player in this game. We miss you when you are gone.

Ironically, I had the same feelings as a child. I wasn't enough. As I described earlier, I was a fat little girl. My dad didn't cope with my weight for most of my life. As an adult, I could manage him. As a child, it just hurt.

My best friend growing up, Stacy, was a tiny little nugget. She was absolutely adorable.

We grew up in the back of a Suburban truck together while our parents raced at the track. We have been friends for more than 40 years.

Stacy would come over to play and my dad would spin her

in circles on the front lawn. I would say, "Daddy, Daddy, my turn, my turn!" His response was, "I can't spin you. You're too big. That would break my back."

Al's Wisdom: Choose your words wisely. Feel first. Speak second.

I admit there was probably some truth in that. And he didn't have the intention of hurting me at all. But it did. It hurt me more than he would ever know.

The more I worried about my weight, the more I gained. I was a latchkey kid for awhile. I coped with the fear of being home alone, the loneliness, and the boredom by eating anything that was available.

One day I ate an entire jar of peanut butter. Well, almost an entire jar. I left one spoonful at the bottom. My dad came home and went to the kitchen to get some peanut butter. He knew how much there was in the jar from the night before. He asked me to come to the kitchen. He said, "What happened to the peanut butter?" I remember thinking, "What a dumb question. He knows what happened to it. I ate it!" I just looked at him and didn't answer. He said, "Do you know what's in this jar? Fat. Lots of fat. Look at the list of ingredients.

You ate an entire jar of fat. Fat makes you fat. Is that what you want?" I just put my head down and said, "No."

It didn't help. His words made things worse. I ate more. I would sneak it. I would eat in shame and disgust. I hated myself, more and more each day.

Al's Wisdom: Our children are helping us heal the wounds of our past. They show us another perspective. They give us the opportunity to see ourselves through the eyes of love. They are allowing us to revisit our pain and choose love. Love for ourselves. Love for each other. Choose love.

As time went on, he never let it go. It was one of the biggest challenges in our relationship for our entire relationship. He always had something to say. Some words of advice on how to lose weight. He always positioned it around health, but I knew he was embarrassed, disappointed, and frustrated. I felt it.

I remember losing a bunch of weight around my 21st birthday. I went over to his house and he said, "You look really good." I was dressed in a cute blouse and shorts. I had mixed feelings. I was so happy to finally feel accepted and acknowledged and at the same time I was so pissed that I had to lose weight to feel that way with my father. I left his house smiling and by the time I drove to the end of the street I was full of tears, sadness, and anger.

I was constantly seeking his approval on my looks and angry when he gave it. Many years were wasted talking about, worrying, obsessing, and crying over weight. Probably the only regret I will die with: wasting so much thought and time on my weight.

The irony is that my father experienced the same thing with his own father. He was so angry with his father for always commenting on his weight.

Al's Wisdom: Our actions are often a reflection of our greatest fears. When we check our intentions and act from love, many of our biggest challenges fade away.

My dad knew my pain.

On the eve of my junior year in high school, he witnessed that pain in full force. I was getting everything together for the first day of school and I broke down in tears. He heard me crying and came into my room.

He asked what was wrong. I couldn't tell him. I was ashamed, embarrassed, humiliated. I cried harder. Beyond the ugly cry. I could tell he was nervous and unsure of how to proceed.

I confessed. I told him, "I can't ride on that bus one more time. I can't do it." He was unaware of the abuse I endured.

Every. Single. Day.

As I would get on the bus the kids would taunt, "Hold on everyone, the whale is getting on. Hold onto your seats, the bus is going down!" On the ride home, the local drug dealer in our school would sit down in the seat in front of me and say, "You know you don't want to be a fat ass. I have some pills that will make you pretty."

I couldn't do it anymore. 10 years was enough.

I was so close to driving. My birthday was only a month and a half away after school started. I already had my car parked in the driveway. I was ready to go.

My dad looked me in the eyes and said, "How can I help?" I knew what I wanted. I couldn't muster up the courage to ask. I wanted him to drive me to school every morning until I got my license. It was a big ask. He stayed up until 3 or 4 a.m., yes, watching tv. I had to be out the door by 6:30 a.m. to get to school. He didn't have to be to work until 9 a.m. I couldn't ask.

I just looked at him and said, "There's nothing you can do."

He said, "What if I took you to school in the morning? Could you find a ride home from a friend? What if I took you to school until you get your license?"

I couldn't believe it. I didn't have to ask. He knew what he needed to do. He was willing to do anything to help me. He was my champion.

He knew that I was on the edge. He knew this was a plea for help. A teenager experiencing a tremendous amount of bullying that needed a break. I still believe he saved me that night. In so many ways, he saved me.

And for the next month and a half, he rolled out of bed at 6 a.m., even when he went to bed at 3 a.m., got his gym clothes together, dropped me off at school, and went to the gym before work. He never complained. He never used it against me. He just did what he had to do to help his little girl get through this thing we call life.

He trusted me. He believed me. He held me in greatness … always.

Al's Wisdom: Sometimes terrible things happen to us to allow the opportunity for someone to show up and shine the light so bright the darkness fades away. They show up to remind you of your greatness, support you in your challenges, and offer help to remind you of your worth on this planet. To remind you of your greatness, especially when you forget. Allow them to show up, great miracles happen when we welcome them in.

He was pretty easy going with me as a teenager. I really didn't have a curfew. My dad would just ask me where I was going and what I was doing. I would let him know when I thought I would be home and I made it a point to be home at the time I agreed to.

I was over at my boyfriend's house on a Friday night. We started a movie later than normal and we both fell asleep. I jumped off the couch and looked at the clock. It was 3:30 in the morning. My boyfriend didn't have a phone in his house and I knew my dad would be panicking. (This was long before cell phones.)

I jumped in my car and sped home. I ran into our apartment and found him sitting in the living room on the phone with the hospital. He dropped the phone and ran to me, grabbed me and squeezed so tight. He said, "Where have you been? What happened? Why would you do this to me?"

I cried and said, "Dad, I promise I fell asleep at Nash's house and I just woke up. I was going to stop and call you from a pay phone but I didn't want to get out of my car at this time of night. I am so so so sorry!! I didn't mean to, I promise. I would never do that to you."

He looked at me with tears in his eyes and said, "I am so thankful you are ok. I love you Doodle. I don't know what I would do without you in my life. You are my world."

And that was it. It was over. No punishment. No lecture. Just a heartfelt reminder of my value in his world. He thought the best of me even when he had plenty of reasons to think the worst.

When I went to my boyfriend's house, I set an alarm from that day on. Just in case. I never wanted my father to have that feeling again.

Al's Wisdom: When we hold each other in love and light, we know there is more to the story than meets the eye. Our minds take over when our hearts need to hold space. Space for love to show up in mysterious ways. Believe in each other. Hold space for love.

Over the next few years, he continued to hold me in greatness. I was working for the MGM Grand Hotel and Casino as a youth counselor. We had children from around the world come in our facility to play and learn while their parents gambled in the casino.

It was a great position, but it barely paid my bills and it was a typical "college job." I was attending college at the time, but I was miserable. I was an excellent student, I just hated taking courses I had no interest in at all. I wanted to start a pre-school. That was my big dream. I had no idea where to start.

I researched options and decided to buy a house at 19 years old, and start an in-home daycare. My Grandma Hazel, in all her greatness, gave me 25 thousand dollars to buy a house and make my dreams come true.

I found a house, back when they would offer loans with no qualifying as long as you had a big chunk of money to invest. I bought it and started the process to get my license. There were so many roadblocks to obtaining an in-home daycare license, I just quit. I continued to work at MGM and decided to finish college.

My dad called me, out of the blue, and asked me to stop by his house after work. When I walked in, he handed me a big thick three-ring binder titled, "How to Run a Daycare." (He bought it off of a late night infomercial.) I chuckled and asked why he bought it.

He said he had been looking in the paper for pre-schools for sale. He found one and wanted to take me to look at it. I was in complete shock and disbelief. How did he think I would be able to open a school with no formal education? Where would the money come from to get the school going? Nothing but questions circled in my head.

I didn't ask any questions. I just said YES.

Al's Wisdom: The forces of love will always create a road to your heart's desire. There is a collective force of light making sure you have everything you need to succeed. Please say yes. Yes to you. Yes to us. Yes to life. Everything is here, waiting for you to say yes. All you have to do is say yes.

We went to look at the school. It wasn't in the best condition or in the best neighborhood, but I gave it a chance. We toured the school and it was pretty run down inside too. We made our way around the entire school. He stopped at the front, looked at me in the eyes, and said, "Well, Doodle, do you think you can do something with this?"

I looked around, paused, and said, "Yep! I can make this work."

He said, "Ok, let's do it."

And that was the beginning of See World Learning Center. I sold my house. He gave me another 17 thousand dollars, and I put the down payment on the school.

I was so scared. I was only 21 years old. The childcare licensing board required a bachelor's degree and I was only in my second year of college. The seller decided she wanted more money for the property and raised the asking price after we put money down. It was all so complicated and yet it all worked out in a beautiful way.

The senior licensing agent really liked me and put an entire portfolio of my work together for the board to see. I stood in front of the entire board and told them why I was the best person to open this school. I was granted a license on the spot.

My dad went to the bank and took all the money he had off his credit cards to pay the difference she was requesting.

Against all odds, I opened the school in April of 1995.

Al's Wisdom: You have the right to get everything you desire in this lifetime. You don't have to prove yourself to get it. You don't have to earn it. All you have to do is show up in love. Love with yourself. Love with life. Love for each other. Show up in love.

My dad and my uncle (his poker buddy and best friend of more than 40 years) sent me a beautiful plant on the first day I opened the doors at See World Learning Center. In the card he wrote, "We are so proud of you. I know that you will change the lives of so many children. I love you so much."

He believed in my dream, even when I didn't think it was possible. He believed in me. He knew that I would fly. He never doubted me. He never questioned me. He just held me in light and love and trusted that I would make magic. And I did.

He invested everything he had in that school. All his money, all his trust, and even his time. I had an employee that needed Monday mornings off so he would come in on his day off from his job to help me in the school. He loved being there. He loved watching me shine. He loved being a witness to my success. He was so proud.

Al's Wisdom: Some of the greatest moments in our lives are watching the ones we love succeed. Bask in the love together. Give each other the appreciation our hearts desire. Risk looking silly, feeling vulnerable, laughing uncontrollably. The benefits far outweigh the risks.

Over the years his health began to decline at a rapid pace.

He had battled diabetes in his late 20's and suffered terrible side effects from the disease. In Grandpa Ralph's chapter I briefly explained the loss of his eyesight. He endured numerous laser surgeries that helped, but now it was catching up with him fast.

He completely lost feeling in his feet from diabetic neuropathy. I knew it was painful, but never realized the extent until our wedding. In everyday life he wore special shoes to support his feet. When he rented his tux and shoes for the wedding, they gave him the standard dress shoes. He wore those shoes the entire day. By the end of the wedding he could barely stand. I later found out from his girlfriend that she begged him to change his shoes, but he refused. He didn't want to embarrass me and ruin my wedding with his ugly shoes. That's what kind of father he was. I never knew. He never complained.

A couple of years passed by and he suffered a heart attack, leading him down a road he would never fully recover from. He had a quadruple bypass, two pacemakers implanted, toes amputated, and eventually his leg amputated.

Watching my dad suffer terrible surgeries and horrific hospital stays took a toll on my spirit. I begged him to see a holistic chiropractor that helped me heal over the years. He refused. He only believed in Western health care.

Everything else was woo woo medicine.

After he had his leg amputated, he fell into a coma. It technically wasn't a coma in the medical world, but he was completely unresponsive. He spent a couple of months in the ICU.

I visited him one afternoon with my brother-in-law, Keith (Brian's brother). I was holding his hand and talking with him about our day. I felt his energy. I knew he wanted to talk about something that mattered.

At this point in time, he was in and out of consciousness. He opened his eyes and didn't use many words. He just looked at me with a tear rolling down his cheek.

I said what my heart told me to say. "Dad, please know how much I love you. I am so so so sorry you are going through this. This is not what we planned. I know this is so hard on you. Please know that I love you and will love you forever. If you want to leave this body, I understand. I will be ok. I will miss you more than you will ever know. I would be so sad, but I am more sad watching you suffer and lose hope. You watched Papa Bill suffer. This is the last thing I want for you. I will honor whatever you want to do. I love you and want you to have peace."

Just tears.

He turned his head over to look at Keith and said, "Will you miss me?"

Keith and I both lost it. I realized in that moment all he wanted to know was, "Did I matter?" Keith, in his greatness, said, "Yes Al, I will miss you. I didn't have to love you. I chose to love you. I will miss you terribly."

Al's Wisdom: You matter more than you know. You are influencing more love, kindness, and courage on this planet by being you. You are so loved and cherished. Your presence is needed. Your light matters.

A week later I received a phone call from the hospital. My sister-in-law, Missy (Brian's sister), was visiting my dad. He asked her to call me. He got on the phone and said, "I'm ready. I'm ready to go be with mom and dad. I want to go home."

Al's Wisdom: We have choice, every step of the way. The choice is always your own.

And with that, I made the call to the hospital. They took him off the cocktail of 37 medications and called in hospice.

We took an ambulance ride to the same hospice my Grandpa Ralph passed away in five years before. We were back. So soon. Unbelievable.

My dad's room was three doors down the hall from where my grandfather took his last breath.

The next few weeks were filled with so many challenging and enlightening experiences. The doctors told me he was suffering from delusions and paranoia. I knew it was more than that.

He would have what I call "experiences." He would call me and say, "I'm going to pick you up in the Corvette and take you for a drive. Meet me at the 7-11 on the corner by the beach." I usually entertained his idea and agreed to meet him. He would call me later and say, "Wasn't that the best ride?" He would start to describe the ride in detail, more detail than he was physically aware of. Brian and I moved in the middle of his hospitalization, so he never visited our current apartment on the beach. Even though he had no idea where we lived, he described it to a tee.

Al's Wisdom: There is so much more to "reality" than we can physically see. There are experiences waiting. They are waiting for us to be open to the possibility that it can happen. To be open to the wonder and magic that is right here, right now. I had to "suffer" to be open to the possibility that I can have experiences that my mind can't explain, but my heart can feel.

He called me in the middle of the night during the week. I was startled because he was whispering. I immediately asked him if he was ok. He responded with, "My dad is standing next to my bed. I'm scared." Again, his father passed away five years prior.

It scared him because he didn't believe in the afterlife (at least in this physical body). He reiterated over and over again, throughout my life, that once we leave this body we are worm food. That's it. Lights out. Party is over.

He was not a religious or spiritual man. He described himself as an agnostic. He was not a believer in much. Death was the end.

So, when his father "visited" him, he was spooked. Big time.

I told him to talk to his dad and ask him why he was there. As I patiently waited on the other end of the phone line, I heard him say, "Dad, Dad, DAD!!! Why are you here?" He came back on the phone with me whispering, "He's not answering me."

We went back and forth for almost 30 minutes. My dad couldn't hear him. Then my dad said, "He's walking to the end of the bed and looking at me. He's leaving now, waving for me to come. I don't want to go Doodle, I don't want to go."

I told him he didn't have to go. I said, "You can stay. It's okay."

He was so sad to see his father go.

Al's Wisdom: We are not on the "other side." We are right here with you, all the time. We never leave you. We are here. When you close your eyes, put your hand on your heart, call our name, feel our presence. We are with you, holding you and loving you forever.

A couple of days later, I had a strong intuitive hit to go see him for the day. (I lived in Northern California at the time and I was flying back and forth to Las Vegas so I could care for my dad. I usually stayed with Keith for weeks at a time so I could take care of him, but I had to go back to work.) He didn't know I was coming. I wanted to surprise him.

I was walking into the hospice and my phone started ringing. I passed by his nurse and she said, "Wow! I didn't know you were coming in today. He just asked for his phone to call you. He will be so happy."

Al's Wisdom: Follow your intuition. It's serving you. Always.

I walked into his room and he looked up with the phone on his ear. I said, "Hello!!!" He looked at the phone, looked at me, and said, "How did you do that?" (He thought I transported through the phone.)

He said, "I was calling you because I have to tell you what happened. It was a miracle. It was amazing. You have to hear it! How did you know to come today?"

I smiled and said, "I just had a feeling I needed to come see you. I wanted to surprise you. And I'm so glad I listened!"

He said, "You're going to need to sit down for this." I pulled a chair up next to his bed and told him, "I'm all yours."

He started to describe, what we call now, his "Day of Enlightenment."

"Doodle, it was the most wonderful, beautiful place. I was wrapped in a cocoon of love and taken to a place that was more than love. It was a place that was indescribable love. There were so many colors and smells, and a feeling of love, but it was more than love. There are no words in our vocabulary to describe it."

He went on and on. He told me that what I believed was true. He apologized for disregarding my beliefs for so long. I was in complete shock initially. I started to feel what he was saying. It was directly from his heart, not his head.

He was full of wonder and light. Love and compassion. Truth and understanding. He was finally enough. More than enough. He was pure light and love. He even said his only regret was not going to see my chiropractor.

I couldn't believe it. He was so clear. Articulate. Authentic. Aware.

He asked the chaplain to come to his room at the end of our conversation. He told her he was ready to go. He wanted to kiss his daughter on the forehead and go be with his parents.

Before I left for the night, he told me that he wanted a way to communicate with me when he died. He knew I loved license plates. He knew all the stories and times when I witnessed a Texas license plate from my grandma and mom. He said, "You know, I think I can do the license plate thing. I can send you a license plate to let you know I am here with you."

With tears rolling down my face, I agreed.

Al's Wisdom: There are so many signs that show up for you everyday. When you begin to notice them, they will multiply. They will surprise you, make you cry, they will make you laugh, and most of all they will remind you that you are never alone. They are the pieces of the puzzle that you desperately need to see the entire picture of life. Ask for a sign when you are in need, it will appear, instantly. All you have to do is ask.

A couple of days went by, and I felt a strong urge to call my dad. It was really late at night, so I wasn't sure I would be able to talk to him. I had the nurse go to his room and help him answer the phone.

He said, "Hi Doodle, I'm not going to be able to talk to you on the phone anymore. I'm going on a mission, like in space. I love you Doodle, so much."

I figured he was just going on another "trip" and said, "Ok dad, have a good time, I love you!"

The next morning I received a phone call from the hospice. My father left this planet for his "mission."

Al's Wisdom: This life we live on planet Earth is so beautiful. And, there is so much more to come. This is not the end. There is no end. Only "to be continued." Stay tuned. There is more to come.

I called the crematorium again. The fourth time in eight years. My mom, Grandpa Ralph, Grandma Pat, and now my dad. It was surreal. How did this happen? Why did this happen? It was too much.

My dad wanted his ashes spread with my grandparents in the ocean. (In hindsight, I would never agree to this again. It was more painful than I ever imagined. Reliving all of their deaths at once was pain that was almost too much to bear. And, the ashes are far from what the movies describe. There are bone fragments and various colors. All too disturbing for me.)

We chartered a boat and had a small ceremony. My family was officially gone. Brian, Keith, and Missy joined me along with my dad's best friend, Uncle Ronnie.

On the day of the ceremony, Missy realized she forgot her shoes. She wanted to run to Target to get a pair before we left.

I was so angry. I didn't want to miss our boat to spread

the ashes. I couldn't believe how selfish she was being. She promised to get back in time.

Brian and Keith went with her to make sure we weren't late for the boat. They pulled into Target, right when they opened at 8 a.m., and parked next to a car with a license plate that read,

LOVE4AL

That's when I knew. I knew he was with me. Loving me. Reminding me of the "cocoon of love." He let me know … all is well.

Al's Wisdom: We are here to love and be loved. All roads lead to love. The suffering I experienced, led me to love. The sadness I felt, led me to love. The sickness I endured, led me to a cocoon of love. It was all worth it. It was so perfectly orchestrated, played, and applauded. We would never know the glory of love without the contrast. This life was magical. See the magic. Feel the love. Your cocoon is here, climb in, you won't regret it. Promise.

THE ROUNDTABLE

The Roundtable:
Papa Bill
Grandma Hazel
Grandpa Ralph
Grandma Pat
Mom
Dad

They all left. I felt like a 37-year-old orphan. Alone. With each death, I lost a piece of my soul. It created a void in my spirit that couldn't be filled. I did my best to move on after each death, but as the years passed and each family member left, it was unbearable.

I often thought of leaving, too.

I couldn't imagine life without my mom and dad. I wanted to watch them be amazing grandparents. I wanted to share vacations together. I wanted to take my dad to all the "Diners, Drive-Ins & Dives" that were featured on his favorite tv show. I wanted to take my mom to all the craft festivals and street fairs that Northern California had to offer.

I wanted to leave. The pain was too much.

But I knew I had work to do here on the planet. I had books that needed to be published, speeches that needed to be delivered, products that needed to be created, and stories I had to tell. (Some of the stories I didn't even know I had to tell, like this one.)

I wanted to stay and play with my husband. We had so many dreams that were yet to be fulfilled. I wanted a family. I knew I was destined to be a mama on this planet to so many children. I knew there was a special soul that needed me. Specifically me, to be his mama.

I did my best to fill the void. Food. Shopping. Friends. Work. Therapy. Vacations. Every attempt to fill the void acted as a temporary Band-Aid. I felt good in the moment. But when I was quiet and still, the silence brought me right back to the pain. The sadness. The grief. The loss.

I was making it through life. Existing. Doing the day in and day out routine required to survive. I definitely had great moments, but there was always this lingering feeling of sadness. My family wasn't there to enjoy the moments with me. I felt hopelessly lost without them.

When we brought our son home, I made an effort to stay connected to my family through spirit. I would see a license plate, hear a song, run into an old friend of my mom's, and point out every Corvette on the road to Jacob. In my effort to stay connected, I actually felt more sadness, grief, and loss. I was constantly aware that they were not here to play with my son, to hold him, or shower him with hugs and kisses. As time passed, my light was going dim.

Five years passed since my father left. I was sifting through my emails and ran across an invitation to a woman's spiritual retreat in Sedona, Arizona. The retreat was focused on reconnecting to the divine feminine. Really, I just wanted to have a girl's weekend with some amazing soulful women.

It wasn't the right time. I didn't have the extra money to go, a caregiver for my son, or even a car to get there.

I let it go.

But the Universe, in all its wisdom, had another plan for me.

My soul sister and dear friend, Taryn, received the same email. She called me up and said, "You are going. Tracy (our dear friend) and I are making sure you are there with us."

I knew I wasn't going to the retreat. No money. No retreat. I humored her with, "Ok, we will see."

I planned to gracefully bow out, but that didn't happen. Taryn and Tracy made sure everything was paid for. My husband was on board to care for our son. My brother-in-law even gave me his brand new Mustang to drive to Sedona.

My angels, in heaven and on earth, made sure that everything was taken care of for me. It was uncomfortable, at times embarrassing, and probably the most vulnerable I have felt in years.

It was meant to be.

We spent the first night at the retreat in bliss. It was such a beautiful experience, surrounded by amazing woman in love and light. After a beautiful opening ceremony, we were told that breath work was on the agenda in the morning and to be ready for an experience.

Oh … it was an experience.

When I arrived in the morning, I immediately grabbed a spot on the floor next to Taryn and Tracy. As I started to set up my space, I heard a nagging voice telling me to get up and move across the room, next to the door. I wanted to ignore the voice, but it got louder. I listened, reluctantly, and found a place by the door to settle in and begin my journey.

I had experienced breath work before. I thought I knew what I was in for, a little relaxation and, if I was lucky, maybe I would have a beautiful vision.

I was on top of a big thick pile of blankets, pillow under my head, ready to begin. The music started and the facilitators guided us into conscious breath. I remember feeling a sense of calmness and peace wash over my body. I was light. Free.

Breath work can trigger a lot of emotions, and has the potential to encourage their release. All I felt was comfort in the stillness. Peace in the quiet.

Another woman in the group was not having my experience, at all. She started screaming, moaning, and crying hysterically. With every scream, I grew more and more uncomfortable. I quickly became scared. I felt unsafe, vulnerable, and wanted to get out of there as quickly as possible. (I was ready to roll up all my stuff and roll out!)

I started praying for protection. Begging for help.

I heard, "We are here for you."

With my eyes closed and my heart open, I felt the presence of my entire deceased family come through the door, single file, and form a circle around my body.

My Dad was on my right shoulder, my Papa Bill was at my left, my Grandma Hazel on my left side holding my hand, my Grandpa Ralph was sitting by my left foot, my Grandma Pat was sitting by my right foot, and my Mom on my right side holding my hand.

They were there. I didn't have to use my eyes. I only needed my heart to feel them. It was so vivid, so real. I could smell them, feel them, and hear their voices as if they were physically in the room.

I cried. I sobbed. I listened.

It was so calming and comforting, I didn't know what to say or do. I just stayed quiet and waited. Waited to hear their message.

My Papa Bill started the dialogue. He said, "We are here for you. We want to explain why we chose you, why we are a family, and the meaning behind all of this."

He continued, "I am the head of our family, the architect. I had to go first because I had a lot of work to do from the other side. I had to make sure all our timelines and objectives were being met. There is a divine order and I am in charge of the design. I make sure we are all on the same page to accomplish the objectives and encourage the others to change course if we need to make miracles happen. We were here for you. We each had our own individual purpose, but that purpose was centered in you and our need to support your mission, vision, and purpose. "

My Grandma Hazel chimed in, "I was so thankful I pulled the straw to be your Grandma. You are our special soul. You came to deliver a message that will inspire people in ways you can't imagine. I was here to show you how to run the system driven by men and still be a lady. I was here to give you love and affection just because you are you. They thought I was spoiling you. I was. You deserve to get everything you want in life. Everything. No exceptions. No apologies. No explanations. Everything. My mission was to remind you how to see yourself in power, bravery, and love. I was a constant reminder that you are worthy of love and everything you desire because you were born. Simply because you were born."

She passed the torch to Grandpa Ralph. He coughed a little to clear his throat and said,

"I'm really sorry I had to be who I was in your life. I didn't want to be mean and hurt you. I had to bring criticism, cruelty, disappointment, disapproval, judgment, and selfdoubt to you. We had this mapped out and contracted long before we came into our bodies. You have so many people that adore you and truly think you are a miracle. We knew, beforehand, you would need contrast in your life. I had to bring the contrast and remind you that the people of the world, including your family, are not telling you who you are. YOU are telling you who you are. I had to be the person to stand up in our family and say, "you're not enough" so you would love yourself even when your own family couldn't love you the way you needed to be loved. I was the one to remind you to hold on to your greatness and keep shining, especially when it feels like you are all alone. I am so sorry for the hurt and pain. I knew you were going to be on the world's stage, you are ready for anything that comes your way. I will be cheering you on and loving you."

Grandma Pat smiled big and said, "We love you more than

you can imagine. I chose to be a writer, a really amazing writer, so you would know and believe it was in you too. I didn't go to college because I wanted you to know that you could be wildly successful without a college degree. I was. I wanted you to know that when they say, "you can't" you actually can, you just have to figure out another way around, go in the backdoor. Your opportunities are endless. You have the world in your hands. Know that my silence over the years was simply to be quiet and bask in your love. I loved feeling your spirit in the room. You are breathtaking, in so many ways. You were everything I wanted in a granddaughter. Our time together was the highlight of my life. Write. Speak. Live, my darling. You are meant for greatness."

My mom looked at Grandma Pat with tears in her eyes and said, "Oh Headie, you are the reason, not a reason, the reason. The reason we came together as a family. We knew that you were destined for greatness and you would need a strong foundation to get you there. We came together to support you in your mission on this planet. We all had our roles. Mine was to love you, to remind you of your greatness especially when the world knocks you down. I am always by your side, every step of the way. I show up in license plates to let you know I am traveling in front of you, behind you, and beside you … always. I am your biggest cheerleader, your devoted fan, and your loving mother…

always. When you lose faith, I am the whisper in your ear that says, 'Just one more time, just get up one more time. We only have love for you.' I will never leave your side. Never."

My dad completed the circle by saying, "Doodle, you are more than a light worker on this planet. You were chosen to share this message and so many more messages to help the world feel good, see greatness, experience compassion, and feel love, deep love, again. I was here to help you have everything you needed to make your magic and miracles happen. I am still here. I am always working to make sure you have everything you need to spread the word. You are the light that lights up life. I was there to ask you the hard questions and inspire you to shine bright. I was there to remind you to be fierce. To stand up for what you believe in, even if you are standing alone. You have done so much and have so much more to come. I am with you along the way, making sure the right license plate shows up for you so you can 'hear me' and know that I am with you every step of the way. I am lining it all up so it's an easier journey. I'm giving you every shortcut I have. When you experience them, know that's me helping you and loving you. I miss our dinners together. Soon enough, we will eat together again. I love you Doodle."

I cried tears that had been waiting to come out for years.

Stuffed down in the depths of my soul.

I didn't want it to stop. I sensed our time was limited. I had so many questions and wanted to hear their wisdom from the other side.

They continued to share the ways they had helped me over the years from the "other side." They even shared the details on how they worked together to coordinate a very difficult international adoption for our son.

They whispered in the foreign doctor's ear, "She's okay, she is just very nervous" when my blood pressure was too high during our mandatory physical for adoption.

My mom had our driver go a specific way so we would pass by "Mary's Chocolate" (the only English words on a shop throughout the entire city).

My Grandma Pat was in charge of our paperwork. And when they required a last minute "education requirement" my Grandma arranged for it to happen quickly and efficiently.

My dad strategically placed a "Las Vegas" tourist bag on a homeless person to let us know he was there and helping us along the way.

My Grandma Hazel made sure we were booked at a luxury hotel, with a discount provided by our beautiful friend Dee, and a restaurant with a Texas theme. My mom and Grandma worked together on this one. There was even a Texas license plate in the restaurant.

My Grandpa Ralph made sure all of the interpreters where clear on our needs and requests. He helped them understand and communicate clearly with us.

My Papa Bill coordinated the entire event. He was orchestrating everything in perfect timing so we could get our son home.

They all worked together to bring Jacob home safe and sound. They gave us constant reminders we were not alone. Reminders that we were being guided and cared for throughout the entire process.

They whispered in the immigration officer's ear, "All the paperwork is there. Welcome Jacob to America. Welcome him home."

We welcomed Jacob home.

In between the tears, they said I would write a book about this experience. It would be a book for the masses, a best seller. They said the story had to be told. It was part of our family's journey. We went through all of this to share it with the world. To help others on their journey. To see how love shows up in so many ways. And to appreciate the experience of life for exactly what it is, an experience. We are in this together.

Our time was coming to an end. They asked me if I had any more questions they could answer. I immediately thought of a question that had haunted me for years: what about my weight? (Really, for the love of God, I have all the wisdom in the world right in front of me and I ask about my weight!)

They all laughed, after all that had been said, I ask about weight. I was quickly informed that the weight was there on purpose. I was like a bear in hibernation. I needed the extra weight to get through a very busy time coming my way.

They also said that we have yet to accept a Universal Truth on this planet. We all have the ability to spontaneously heal. We have the power to ask our bodies to heal, and they will honor the request.

I asked for a healing. And one by one they covered me in blankets of love. It's a challenge to describe, because each family member gently placed what can only be described as layers of love around my body.

It was a feeling beyond peace. Magical.

They wanted me to understand and be completely clear. They were not doing the healing, they were simply adding love to amplify my own body's natural healing powers. Just add love.

The idea of spontaneously healing was difficult for me to wrap my brain around. It certainly isn't the most popular or professed belief in our society. But something happened.

When I was "wrapped in love," I felt it. I felt the power of my body to take care of itself in a beautiful way. I felt the love infuse in my body and spirit. I felt relaxed. Healthy. Vibrant. At ease. I felt alive!

We all have the ability to heal ourselves when we ask and feel the love.

Time was passing at warp speed. At least it felt like it. I couldn't get enough. The music was coming to an end, the facilitators started to bring us back to awareness.

The tears were falling faster. I begged … please don't leave me, not again.

They said, "We are with you, always." My Papa Bill piped up and said, "Well we aren't with you always. Your mom, she is always with you. But we travel around."

They quickly followed with, "We are with you when you call. All you have to do is say "roundtable" and we will circle you and support you. Say "roundtable" and we are here. Instantly."

They left as they came in … single file. The music faded, the facilitators welcomed us back from our experience, and I felt a peace that can't be described. I sat down to eat lunch with Taryn and shared the story. She looked at me and said, "You have to write this book!"

I shared it with the entire group of women, the reaction was the same, "You have to write this book."

Months have gone by. I didn't think I could write this book. I had no idea what it was going to be about. The only direction my family gave me was each member would have a chapter, there would be an introductory chapter and a roundtable chapter to complete the book.

I was struggling to sit down and do it. I had no clue what to write. I called Taryn and she said, "Just sit down and write. They will help you do it. I will be your accountability buddy. Send me a chapter by Monday."

I called a roundtable.

I cried and asked for help.

I sat down at my computer on Sunday night at 11 p.m., staring at a blank page with a blinking curser, two candles burning, pictures of each family member displayed, and said, "Ok, I'm here. I'm ready."

I started typing. And didn't stop until 4 a.m.

I did it over and over for the next 13 days.

This book was meant to be. It came in so fast, so effortless (except for my mom, that chapter was brutal to write). Completed in two weeks.

Just as a point of reference, my first book that I co-authored with Taryn Voget, "How to Raise a Happy Child (and be happy too)", required a year and a half investment of time, energy, and love.

As I come to an end with this book, I feel the same way as when they all left that day at the retreat. I don't want it to end.

This book has given me the opportunity to see love when all I could see (and feel) was pain. It has allowed me to step back and hear the truth from the other side. I finally stopped crying. Started breathing. Feeling. I felt a peace that I have never felt.

I asked my mom when I was done writing her chapter, "Am I going to die after this book? It feels like my whole life has been for this book. It feels like I'm all done."

She replied, "No sweetheart, you are not going to die. You are finally going to live." Mother's Day was a few days ago. It was the first Mother's Day I didn't cry the entire day, feeling sad, missing her. For the first time, I felt at peace, safe in the arms of love.

And with that, I thanked her. I thanked all of them for showing up. And for being the most amazing family. For teaching me there is so much more to all that we experience, everything is here for our highest good. Everything is here to serve us. Everything.

We are connected in wisdom and love. It's not your wisdom or their wisdom. It's our wisdom. A collective wisdom.

They are there. Waiting for us to ask. Waiting to wrap us in love.

All we have to do is ask.

ABOUT HEATHER

I've always thought that my soul's calling, my entire purpose on this planet, was to be a voice for children and an inspiration to parents. My life, my world, has been centered on bridging the communication and connection gap between adults and children. The past 25 years has gifted me with the opportunity to work with over 30,000 kids.

When I was 21 years old, my father believed in my dream to open a one-of-a-kind preschool where children were empowered, celebrated for their unique gifts, and loved beyond words. My family contributed time, energy, and money to make this dream a reality and See World Learning Center was born in Las Vegas, Nevada.

For nearly a decade, I raised a generation of children who believed they were a gift to the world, and taught them how to share their gifts with others. My husband and I fostered many children over the years. All of these amazing kids had so much to teach me about how to communicate, cooperate, and connect with them in the most loving ways.

Years later, my passion spread to impacting the lives of entire families. I established the Touch of Life Wellness Center, also in Las Vegas. It was a place where people could come for healing, holistic alternatives, and personal transformation. The center gave me a place to explore and embrace the natural healing powers we all possess. It gave me a place to witness and share miracles everyday.

When I was ready to evolve into my next business and life adventure, I sold the wellness center and created a new company that married all the wisdom I gathered from See World and Touch of Life. Because we all have an unbreakable wisdom that resides within, it made sense to start a company that reminded the world of exactly that. WiseInside was born.

My first creation was an award-winning game, WiseTalk for Families, designed to help parents and children share meaningful, heartfelt moments filled with communication, connection, and love.

Next, I was honored to co-author an award-winning book with Taryn Voget from Everyday Genius Institute, How to Raise a Happy Child (and be happy too). Our book has helped thousands of parents tap into their own wisdom and feel good on the journey through parenthood.

Everything I've created has led me here. I never thought in a million years I would be writing a book detailing the conversations I've had with family that has passed on. I guess the universe holds the power to unfold dharma much bigger than our own plans all in perfect time and space.

My eternal family, in all their wisdom, reminded me that my foundation is WiseInside. While encouraging the connection between parents and their children is a big slice of my life's work on this planet, it's been shown to me that this message transcends every niche. There is so much more to each and every one of us than meets the eye. My soul's calling is to remind you all:

You are WiseInside and surrounded by love, always. Promise.

FAMILY PHOTOS

My Dad & Me
Alan Robie

The Corvette
I came home
in from the
hospital
Alan Robie

My Mom
Mary Robie

My
Grandma
Hazel
Hazel
Aumiller

My Papa Bill
& My Mom
William Aumiller

Daisy Mae
(left) &
Furby (right)

My Grandma Pat
& Me
Patricia Robie

Grandma Pat - the only woman at a table full of men in 1951

My Grandpa Ralph
in the hot pink
shirt I gave him
Ralph Robie

My Husband
Brian & Me
Brian Criswell

Meeting Jacob
for the first time
at the adoption
agency

Our Son Jacob
Jacob Criswell

Create Heartfelt Connection in Minutes with WiseTalk for Famlies®

A "tool" for parents and a "game" for children, WiseTalk for Families® builds a communication lifeline that allows you and your child to share meaningful conversations in minutes.

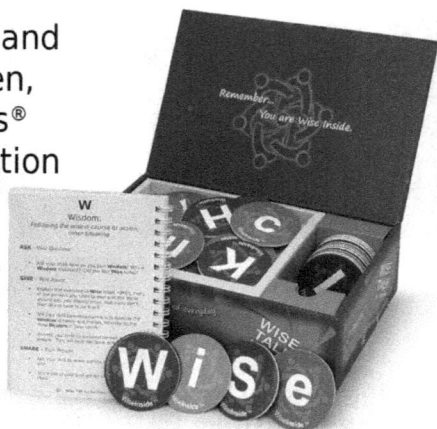

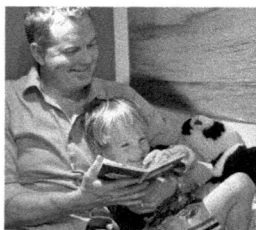

- Meaningfully *connect* with your child every day

- Create quality time for having fun and *communicating*

- Share your *values* with each other

- Learn *what to say and how to say it*

www.wiseinside.com

WiseInside
wisdom shared from the inside out

Also by Heather Criswell

✶ Award Winning ✶

simply *genius* parenting strategies that work

✦ How-to videos included ✦

How to Raise a
Happy Child
(and be happy too)

Heather Criswell, Kid Whisperer
Taryn Voget, Cofounder of the Everyday Genius Institute

available at **amazon**.com

& www.everydaygeniusinstitute.com

ACKNOWLEDGEMENTS

All of this is possible because I am loved.

To my Eternal Family, my Roundtable, I am so thankful for our time on this planet together. I often felt like you all left too early. Now I know you left exactly when you wanted to leave. I used to cry a thousand tears because I missed your laughter, your hugs and kisses, and most of all, our conversations. I don't have to cry anymore. I now know we can have a conversation at any given time. I don't have to wait to see you again on the other side. You are here. Now. I am forever grateful for our family and the love we share. Thank you for reminding me that everything circles back to love.

To my husband, Brian, we have been on this journey so many times together and I am so thankful for your unwavering support and love. After writing this book, I realized we have traveled to hell and back countless times. And even though we experienced the depths of sadness, grief and loss in a short space of time, we are still here. Together. Smiling. Crying. Laughing. Together. Thank you for sharing this life with me and loving me along the way.

To my son, Jacob Alan, I am so thankful you chose me as your mother. I didn't want to stay on this planet when everyone left, until you came. You gave me reason to stay and play. You help me see the world through the eyes of love. You are the brightest light on this planet and my greatest teacher. You amaze me everyday and continue to remind me that love shows up in unexpected ways. You always remind me to circle back to love. I love you more than a gazillion bazillion bright shining stars.

To my soul sister, Taryn Voget, no words can ever describe the love I have for you. You have been my biggest cheerleader, a guide back to sanity when I am so lost, the voice of reason talking me down off the ledge, the friend I call when I need to be reminded of my greatness, and the one I count on to always be there as a force of love. You help me see my genius, because you are a genius. I wouldn't be who I am today without you and your love, a love I have felt deeply through experience. You are one of the greatest gifts of my lifetime. I am forever grateful.

To my Fairy Godmother, Wendy Dearborne, I can't thank you enough for stepping in as a guide, a source of great wisdom, and a mom on this earth. I never have to ask you for help. You are tuned into my well-being. You come before I call. You help before I ask. You give without hesitation. You have been, and continue to be, the greatest source of love and compassion when I feel completely alone on this planet. Thank you for loving me as your own. My heart is always full of your love.

To my SelfLoving friend, Elyse Hughes, I am so thankful I moved back to Vegas, because I now know it was to meet you. I can always count on you to join me in a text conversation while we're working at 3 a.m., to turn my tears into laughter that makes me pee my pants (#forrealzzz), to believe in and inspire me to follow my dreams, to sprinkle your magic word fairy dust on my copy and books, and to spend time in the park, ride bikes with Jakey, and remember what this life is all about. There will never be another Elyse Hughes, I'm so grateful I get to spend this life with you.

To my brother-in-law, Keith, I am so glad you chose to be my brother on this planet. Even though we were not together in the beginning, we will be together to the end. You have been a great source of inspiration and love over the past 19 years. I am so thankful for your support, compassion and love. I can't wait to pick out your Alfa Romeo! I love you and can't wait to share this journey together as a family.

To Stacy, Uncle Ronnie, Sarah, Jenny, Ray, Ruth, all my dear friends, my See World family, my Touch of Life family, and seekers, thank you all for your love and support over the years. Your love is in my soul forever.

To all the children that have graced me with their wisdom and love, I am eternally grateful. You have all reminded me that we come here in love, with love, and for love.

SHARE YOUR STORY

We all have a story.
I would love to hear yours.
Have you experienced connecting with loved ones
who have passed on?
What is the wisdom they shared?

Share your WiseInside moment.
Send your wisdom and love to:

love@wiseinside.com

We come here in Love, with Love, and for Love.

THANK YOU.

Love is here for you...Always.

Promise.

www.ingramcontent.com/pod-product-compliance
Lightning Source LLC
Chambersburg PA
CBHW072344090426
42741CB00012B/2919